YORK NOTES

C000224827

READING SKILLS

REVISION AND EXAM PRACTICE

HELEN STOCKTON

The right of Helen Stockton to be identified as the Author of this Work has been asserted by her in accordance with the Copyright, Designs and Patents Act 1988

Additional material written by Mike Gould

YORK PRESS
322 Old Brompton Road, London SW5 9JH

PEARSON EDUCATION LIMITED
Edinburgh Gate, Harlow,
Essex CM20 2JE, United Kingdom
Associated companies, branches and representatives throughout the world

First published 2017

10 9 8 7 6 5 4 3 2

ISBN 978–1–2921–8635–1

Phototypeset by Carnegie Book Production
Printed in Slovakia

Text credits: Extracts from *An Inspector Calls* by J. B. Priestley (Harlow, UK: Heinemann, 1992). Copyright © J. B. Priestley 1945. Reproduced by permission of Penguin Books Ltd, and United Agents on behalf of the Estate of J. B. Priestley. Excerpts from PIGEON ENGLISH by Stephen Kelman. Copyright © 2011 by Stephen Kelman. Reprinted by permission of Bloomsbury Publishing Plc and Houghton Mifflin Harcourt Publishing Company. All rights reserved. Canadian permission granted by House of Anansi Press, Toronto. Extracts from *Rebecca* and *Jamaica Inn* by Daphne Du Maurier reproduced with permission of Curtis Brown Group Ltd, London on behalf of The Chichester Partnership. Copyright © The Chichester Partnership, 1936. 'The Simple Truth' from THE SIMPLE TRUTH: POEMS by Philip Levine, copyright © 1994 by Philip Levine. Used by permission of Alfred A. Knopf, an imprint of the Knopf Doubleday Publishing Group, a division of Penguin Random House LLC. All rights reserved. 'Fake Smile' by Mike Gould reproduced by permission of the author.

Photo credits: Capture Light/Shutterstock for page 7 middle / KKulikov/Shutterstock for page 7 bottom / V.Belov/Shutterstock for page 8 middle / Mushan/Shutterstock for page 8 bottom / Getty Images Publicity/Getty Images for page 12 middle / Photo 12/ Alamy Stock Photo/Alamy for page 14 bottom / Kaylie_Kell/Shutterstock for page 15 bottom / Joe Gough/Shutterstock for page 16 middle / sysasya photography/Shutterstock for page 18 bottom / Simon Baylis / Alamy Stock Photo/Alamy for page 20 bottom / Raisa Kanareva/Shutterstock for page 21 bottom / vbmark/Shutterstock for page 22 bottom / wavebreakmedia/Shutterstock for page 23 top / Jiri Vaclavek/Shutterstock for page 25 bottom / Yasuhiro amano/Shutterstock for page 27 top / Robin Whalley/Shutterstock for page 29 bottom / Melica/Shutterstock for page 30 middle / robertprzybysz/© iStock for page 32 top / Ollyy/Shutterstock for page 36 bottom / Twinsterphoto/Shutterstock for page 41 middle / nanka/Shutterstock for page 42 bottom / Ricardo Reitmeyer/Shutterstock for page 44 top / kdshutterman/Shutterstock for page 46 middle / Yuriy Chertok/Shutterstock for page 49 top / Michal Durinik/Shutterstock for page 49 bottom / Neil McAllister / Alamy Stock Photo/Alamy for page 52 middle / Marbury/© iStock for page 55 middle / whitemay /© iStock for page 56 middle and page 58 top / 6 Maite De Elias/Shutterstock for page 61 top / IB Photography/Shutterstock for page 66 bottom / Helen Hotson/Shutterstock for page 67

CONTENTS

CHAPTER SIX: PUTTING IT INTO PRACTICE

CHAPTER SEVEN: ANSWERS AND GLOSSARY

1.1 UNDERSTANDING GENRE AND FORM

In both English Language and English Literature GCSEs, you will be required to read critically, interpret ideas and information, and explain how meaning has been created.

ASSESSMENT OBJECTIVES

The objectives in GCSE English Language upon which your reading will be assessed are:

(A01)	• Identify and interpret explicit and implicit information and ideas • Select and synthesise evidence from different texts
(A02)	• Explain, comment on and analyse how writers use language and structure to achieve effects and influence readers, using relevant subject terminology to support their views
(A03)	• Compare writers' ideas and perspectives, as well as how these are conveyed, across two or more texts
(A04)	• Evaluate texts critically and support this with appropriate textual references

These AOs are assessed in short and longer responses to fiction and nonfiction extracts on the exam papers.

In GCSE English Literature, the objectives which relate to how well you respond as a reader are:

(A01)	Read, understand and respond to texts. Students should be able to: • Maintain a critical style and develop an informed personal response • Use textual references, including quotations, to support and illustrate interpretations.
(A02)	• Analyse the language, form and structure used by a writer to create meanings and effects, using relevant subject terminology where appropriate.
(A03)	• Show understanding of the relationships between texts and the contexts in which they were written.

GENRES AND FORMS

You will need to understand the different forms writers use and for what purpose or effect. You will also need to know what is meant by **genre**, what the specific features or constraints of different genres are, and how this influences our understanding of texts.

- **What is genre**? This refers to the type or category of writing, for example, a novel or a poem.
- **What is form**? This applies to the layout or structure of a text, for example, the way a poem is divided into verses.

IDENTIFYING THE FORM OR GENRE

There are many different types or **genres** of texts. Here are some that you are most likely to encounter in your GCSE English Language paper with details of their main **conventions**:

Form or genre	Conventions	Purpose or effect
Formal letter	• Formal opening summarising letter's purpose • Series of key points • Conclusion outlining actions moving forward • Formal sign-off	• To raise an issue or complaint • To communicate concisely the key points • To initiate a clear action in response
Magazine feature	• Focus on a particular topic or subject • Eye-catching title or heading • Presentational devices such as bullet points, sub-headings, pictures with captions • Often, use of direct personal experience or quotations	• To entertain or inform • To attract readers to the article and to engage them in reading the complete piece • To be relevant to the lives and interests of the intended readership
Broadsheet news report or article	• Focus on very recent or topical events • Eye-catching title or heading • Formal language and some factual information • Use of direct experience or quotations	• To inform about a topical issue or event • To provide factual information • To offer information in a balanced, unbiased way, or to offer a particular view, depending on context
Literary non-fiction (e.g. travel writing, diary)	• Literary styles and techniques • Factual information • Personal voice or perspective • Imaginative recreation of real lives, events and experiences	• To gain the reader's sympathy and understanding • To make non-fiction writing easy and engaging to read • To entertain as well as inform
Novel or short story	• Setting, plot, characters, conflict and themes • Prose, often with **dialogue** • Vivid description	• To entertain and inform
Persuasive speech or article arguing a point of view	• Rhetorical questions • Mixture of fact and opinion • Subjective and emotive language • Repetition for emphasis • Inclusive language • Use of **anecdote** or quotations from others • Acknowledgement of counter-argument	• To strongly set out points in support of a particular point of view • To actively engage others in seeing the subject from the same point of view • To get others to take action

❶   Read extracts A, B, C and D and match each one with its genre from page 6.

Extract A

'I am here today to talk to you about the totally inadequate facilities for young, disabled people in the town centre. Have you ever stopped to imagine what it would be like trying to negotiate the old buildings with steps and the high curbs in a wheelchair?'

Extract B

'Then would you like me to be married, Father?' said Eppie, with a little trembling in her voice.

'I'll not be the man to say no, Eppie,' said Silas emphatically, 'but we'll ask your godmother. She'll wish the right thing by you and her son too.'

Extract D

Are holidays at home a thing of the past?

Traditionally quaint or old-fashioned and out-dated?

When was the last time you spent a holiday in the UK? Over recent years, the attractions of the 'staycation' have waxed and waned like the weather.

Extract C

Dear Ms Khan,

I am writing to complain about the changes being proposed to the school uniform.

In the first instance, a formal uniform with blazer style jackets will be more expensive and this will cause unnecessary hardship for families on low incomes.

AIMING HIGH

Using the information in the grid on page 6, can you say which key features or conventions of the particular genre the writers of Extracts A, B, C and D have employed?

APPLYING YOUR SKILLS   A02 A02

❷   Read the following extract. Then write a paragraph explaining which genre it is and the conventions or features that suggest this to you.

After a long plane journey, the first glimpse of the island didn't disappoint. The white sandy beaches and the impossibly blue seas created a vision straight out of a travel brochure.

The airport was clean, the transport to the hotel punctual, relaxed and friendly, as we were embraced by the warm air and balmy breath of Barbados. Palm trees fringed the roads, sugar cane waved tasselled heads from the adjacent fields and the pace of life slowed to the laid-back languor of the Caribbean.

1.2 IDENTIFYING THE PURPOSE AND THEME

As part of your study of both GCSE English Language and English Literature you will have to establish the core purpose of a text or texts, in some cases comparing them.

PRIMARY AND SECONDARY PURPOSES

A writer always has a **purpose** for or reason behind their text. Sometimes this is clear and straightforward and sometimes it is less obvious. The purpose is likely to be one of the following:

- To inform or advise
- To promote something
- To raise awareness or provoke thought through discussion
- To entertain or amuse
- To persuade or to argue a personal viewpoint

Consider the purposes of the following extract from a newspaper article:

Glamping – it's camping, but not as we know it!

Pouring rain, a muddy field, the toilet block miles away, parents arguing because someone had forgotten the tin opener. Yes, these were the joys of camping in my childhood. Maybe you had the same experience? But that has all changed. Now you can stay in elegant tepees with their own log burners and be served a delicious cooked breakfast, as I found out on a recent holiday to Devon...

Writing often has both a **primary** (the main) and **secondary** (less important) purpose. It is useful to understand how these purposes work together. Here, you could argue the main purpose is to persuade the reader that 'glamping' (posh camping) is worth a try.

❶ What evidence is there that the secondary purpose is to amuse or entertain? (Look for vivid description, use of humour, appeals to reader.)

CORE IDEA AND THEMES

If the purpose of a text is the 'why' it has been written, then the core idea and themes are the 'what' it has been written about. A text usually focuses on one main idea and a number of subsidiary ideas that are revisited throughout it: the **themes**. If a text is a piece of fabric, the core idea would be the central colour at the heart of the design, and the themes or key points would be the strands of differing widths and shades, that run through it.

The core idea, especially in nonfiction articles, can often be identified by:

- Checking the title or headline
- Reading the opening and the conclusion

❷ Based on these headlines, what will the core idea of each article be?

A
ROBOTS
FILL THE
SKILLS GAP

B
THE SKY'S
THE LIMIT FOR
NEW AIRBUS

C
TEENAGERS
– DO THEY
REALLY DESERVE
TO VOTE?

IDENTIFYING KEY POINTS

Consider the following extract. A student has identified some of the key points or ideas presented by checking the title and opening and closing paragraphs. What other clues has he/she identified?

High Streets are in decline

Another contributor – large supermarkets taking the place of independent shops

Transport issues add to barriers facing High Streets shops

The Death of the High Street

Take a look at your local High Street and you will see that it is far from the thriving hub of bygone eras. The number of vacant shops with boarded up windows has increased, charity shops have proliferated, pop-up or temporary shops that take advantage of short lets in empty premises, will be in evidence and the remaining shops will be the same old tired chain stores you can find across the country.

One of the reasons for the decline is the out of town superstores, often situated in purpose built retail parks. These attract shoppers away from the town centres with their bewildering range of goods and large, free car parks.

Usually, as part of these shopping emporiums there are vast supermarkets, competing against each other to offer the best food at the cheapest prices, and housing a range of the specialist butcher, bakers, grocers, newsagents, pharmacies and cafes that used to frequent the empty shops on our High Streets.

Charity shops, with their donated goods and volunteer staff have the low overheads necessary to succeed in the old towns, but give a rather run-down jumble-sale feel that deters independent stores. Poor parking, limited public transport and congested roads also contribute to the general malaise. It might not yet be all over for the High Street yet but it requires major change to bring it back to life.

Out-of-town superstores – one contributor to the decline

Charity shops compete unfairly due to their low costs

High streets are endangered but not extinct yet

APPLYING YOUR SKILLS

(A02)

❸ Based on the points made, and looking at the article's title, opening and ending (and any other relevant clues), write a paragraph explaining:

- What the core idea or focus of the text is
- What the primary purpose of the piece is

1.3 UNDERSTANDING AUDIENCE AND READER

In your reading of fiction and non-fiction texts, you may be asked to make a judgement about the effect of a writer's choices on the reader or audience. But what do these terms mean?

AUDIENCE

In order to evaluate the success of the writing, it can be useful to identify who the audience is. Audiences may be defined by some of the following factors:

- Age – e.g. children, students, parents or elderly
- Gender, ethnic or cultural background
- Social or economic background – e.g. linked to level of education, profession, income
- Time period: contemporary audience or audience from a particular period

1 Read the cover blurbs below for three very different books. Who is the book aimed at each case? Match the audience A, B and C below to blurbs 1, 2 and 3.

A Parent or carers of children of either gender, aged four and just about to start nursery education

1 Whether you need to know the best place for lunch in Prague, the cheapest train fare to Paris from Lyon, or how to book a ticket to Barcelona's Parc Guell, *Budget Europe* is the guide for you.

B Young adults, students planning a gap year or extended holiday across Europe

2 It's Minnie Ant's first day at Bug Preschool but she has to pack her bag before she leaves. Can you help her?

C Predominately male, middle-aged or older with sufficient money to pursue such a hobby

3 Dreams of restoring your own vintage MG can become reality thanks to page-after-page of advice, helpful diagrams and tried-and-trusted suppliers' details that lie within.

Now, look at the table on page 11. Knowing your target audience and the subject matter will help you decide on the **style** and **register** of language.

❷ Copy and complete the final column of the table, deciding what sort of language is most appropriate.

Subject matter	Target audience	Form and structure	Language
Changes to school security systems	Headteacher	Letter layout: address of sender on the right and intended recipient on the left, date, correct greeting and sign-off.	formal and polite
The difficulty of children's homework	*The Sunday Times* readers	Newspaper article: headline and sub-headings, pictures with captions	
Review – *Harry Potter and the Cursed Child*	Children, aged 11 plus and adults	Introduction to the play, outline of strengths, outline of weaknesses, conclusion with recommendation	

AUDIENCE AND CONTEXT

Audiences vary over time. For example, you will study works that were written over 400 years ago, like Shakespeare's play, *Macbeth*, in which the main character murders the rightful king but is ultimately defeated. How would Shakespeare's audience have responded differently from one watching the play today? We know that in Shakespeare's time:

- Kings believed they were chosen by God (the Divine Right of Kings)
- The king, James I, was concerned that others wanted the throne: kings had been killed or overthrown in the past
- King James watched the play

❸ Why do you think Shakespeare makes sure Macbeth fails as a king?

❹ Why would Shakespeare's audience be *more affected* by the prospect of a king being killed than an audience today?

> **TOP TIP**
>
> Be sure that you are clear on the difference between an audience and a reader. **Audience** is a collective term for the wider consumer of a text or a performance. **Reader** refers to the specific relationship between the writer and a person reading a text and so has a narrower focus.

APPLYING YOUR SKILLS

Read the following extract from magazine:

> *When was the last time you reviewed your diet? Not the tired New Year's notion of giving up chocolate or drinking more water, but a comprehensive examination of what you eat and drink daily. What do you have for breakfast, lunch and your evening meal? How much do you snack and what on? Are you eating a suitable balance of protein, fat and carbohydrates? There are always food fads, but you need to look at the basics. Try keeping a food diary for a fortnight. You'll be surprised at the results.*

❺ Write a paragraph of 75–100 words about this text and who it is aimed at. Consider:
- What sort of person/people (age, gender etc.) is it aimed at?
- Is it aimed at a specific reader or a general audience?

1.4 FACTS, STATISTICS AND OPINIONS

One of the reading skills required for GCSE English Language is identifying evidence that supports a point of view within a text.

FACTS

A **fact** is something that is generally held to be true and that can be proved, if necessary, using evidence. For example, that man has landed a space craft on the moon is a fact that can be proved by reference to news footage, film, photographs and witness testimony.

STATISTICS

A **statistic** is a type of fact that refers to numerical data about a specific subject. For example, twelve astronauts, in total, have landed on the moon's surface.

❶ Read the passage below and identify the facts and statistics. One example of each has been identified to start you off.

Fact —

Major Tim Peake is the first British Astronaut to go on a space walk. He stayed at the International Space Station, coming back in a Soyuz capsule with two other crew members and touching down in the Kazakhstan Desert. While in space, Tim remotely steered a robot and ran the London Marathon. His mission lasted 186 days, took him on 3,000 orbits of the earth and covered a distance of about 125 million kilometres. He touched back down to earth on the 18th June 2016.

— Statistic

Facts and statistics can be used to support a point of view on a topic. Consider the facts and statistics given for and against space travel in the table below.

For space travel	Against space travel
Human space travel has helped us to find out more about the history of the universe.	The orbiting carbon conservatory that crashed into the Pacific in 2009 cost $278 million.
Space travel expands technology and has created new industries.	'Lunacy' originates from the word 'lunar' or the idea that the moon's gravitational pull adversely affects the mind.
The International Space Station captures 1,000 images a day that help to monitor natural disasters.	A spaceship travelling at a million miles an hour would still take 4,000 years to reach the nearest potentially inhabitable planet.
Space Station educational programmes inspire more than 43 million students across the globe.	A number of unmanned space craft sent to Mars have been lost, costing millions of pounds.

❷ Identify which are the facts and which are the statistics in the above table.

OPINION AND BIAS

When a writer wants to promote a particular point of view, they tend to use the facts and statistics from one side only. This is called using **bias**. In a biased text the writer tries to influence the reader in favour of one case, without attempting to be fair and is also far more likely to use **assertions** (unsubstantiated statements or comments) and opinions.

An **opinion** is a belief, view or judgment about a topic. If others are capable of holding a differing view about a statement, however unlikely, then it is an opinion and not a fact. For example, an older person might hold the opinion that GCSEs were more rigorous in their day than they are now. You might disagree!

❸ Read through the magazine article below and identify whether the highlighted pieces are facts, statistics or opinions. Some of have been done for you.

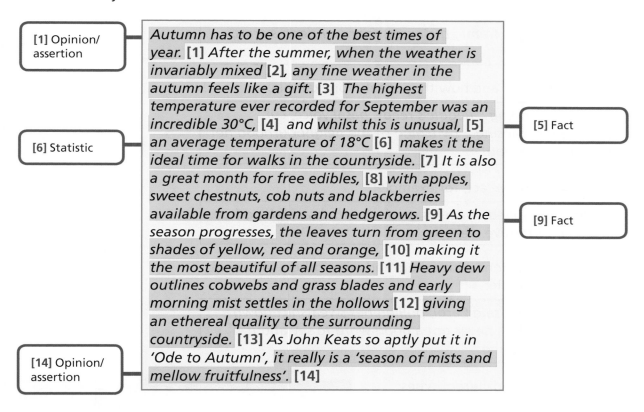

[1] Opinion/ assertion

[6] Statistic

[14] Opinion/ assertion

Autumn has to be one of the best times of year. [1] *After the summer, when the weather is invariably mixed* [2]*, any fine weather in the autumn feels like a gift.* [3] *The highest temperature ever recorded for September was an incredible 30°C,* [4] *and whilst this is unusual,* [5] *an average temperature of 18°C* [6] *makes it the ideal time for walks in the countryside.* [7] *It is also a great month for free edibles,* [8] *with apples, sweet chestnuts, cob nuts and blackberries available from gardens and hedgerows.* [9] *As the season progresses, the leaves turn from green to shades of yellow, red and orange,* [10] *making it the most beautiful of all seasons.* [11] *Heavy dew outlines cobwebs and grass blades and early morning mist settles in the hollows* [12] *giving an ethereal quality to the surrounding countryside.* [13] *As John Keats so aptly put it in 'Ode to Autumn', it really is a 'season of mists and mellow fruitfulness'.* [14]

[5] Fact

[9] Fact

❹ Write a paragraph on whether or not this article presents a balanced view of autumn or a biased one, using evidence from the article.

APPLYING YOUR SKILLS   **A01**

❺ Write a short piece of 100 words, containing facts, statistics and opinion (with some assertions) that suggests autumn is the worst time of year. (Make up the facts or stats if you don't have any to hand!) Then swap pieces with a friend to test your reading skills by:

● Identifying the use of facts and statistics
● Highlighting opinions or assertions

1.5 CHARACTER AND VOICE

The concepts of character and voice are key to the relationship between writer and reader. You will be asked to evaluate how effectively writers use them.

CHARACTER

A character is a participant in a story, created or recreated on the page to embody or communicate a key message from the writer to the reader. **Characterisation** refers to the process of establishing and developing a character within a piece of writing.

Characterisation can be achieved in the following ways:

1 by being told information directly by the writer, for example:

> *Reggie was thin and slightly stooped, with a tattered shirt that was hung rather than worn on his slight frame, the excess fabric under his arms, flapping gently in the breeze.*

2 through what characters say and how they speak, for example:

> *'Oi, what d'y think you're doing?' Reggie's reedy, nasal voice, cut through the Sunday calm, causing a twitching of the neighbourhood net curtains, 'Get lost, the lot of you!'*

3 through how characters move/act, for example:

> *He moved with surprising speed down his garden path, brandishing his wooden broom like an offensive weapon.*

4 through characters' interactions with others and what others say about them in **dialogue**, for example:

> *'Old misery, that's what he is,' said Carol, pulling her sweatshirt down angrily over her leggings. 'He's never got a good word to say about anyone and he's always moaning.'*

Characters can be a number of different types:

The **protagonist** refers to the major or principal character within a story, e.g. In *Jane Eyre*, Jane herself or Elizabeth Bennet in *Pride and Prejudice*.

The **antagonist** is the character that opposes or is the source of conflict and tension with the protagonist, e.g. Mr Rochester or Mr Darcy.

Secondary or **minor characters** are characters that interact with the protagonist and help to advance the story, e.g. Adèle, Mrs Fairfax, Helen Burns, Mrs Reed in *Jane Eyre* or Kitty, Charlotte or Lady Catherine De Burgh in *Pride and Prejudice*.

UNDERSTANDING CHARACTERISATION

Read the following extract from the beginning of *Great Expectations* by Charles Dickens. This is the reader's first introduction to Mrs Joe, the sister of the protagonist, Pip.

As you read, consider the four 'pointers' from page 14 that tell us what a character is like.

> *My sister, Mrs. Joe Gargery, was more than twenty years older than I, and had established a great reputation with herself and the neighbours because she had brought me up 'by hand'. Having at that time to find out for myself what the expression meant, and knowing her to have a hard and heavy hand, and to be much in the*
> 5 *habit of laying it upon her husband, as well as upon me, I supposed that Joe Gargery and I were both brought up by hand [...]*
> *My sister, Mrs. Joe, with black hair and eyes, had such a prevailing redness of skin that I sometimes used to wonder whether it was possible she washed herself with a nutmeg-grater instead of*
> 10 *soap. She was tall and bony, and almost always wore a coarse apron, fastened over her figure behind with two loops, and having a square impregnable¹ bib in front, that was stuck full of pins and needles. She made it a powerful merit in herself, and a strong reproach against Joe, that she wore this apron so much. Though I*
> 15 *really see no reason why she should not have taken it off, every day of her life.*
>
> **Glossary:**
> ¹ *impregnable* – unable to be broken through

We are told the following information about Mrs Joe:

● She is Pip's sister
● She is more than twenty years older than Pip

❶ Find at least three more pieces of information we are told directly about Mrs Joe.

This information is explicit and so is told directly to the reader by the narrator. However, some is shown more indirectly. When this is the case, you must make an **inference** from what is being said. (See also Unit 2.2.)

❷ Look again at the description of Mrs Joe's apron in lines 8 and 9. What does this suggest about Mrs Joe?

VOICE

The **voice** in a piece of writing is the point of view from which the story is being told or the main speaking voice that the reader is listening to.

The story may be told:

- Through a character in the story or
- Through a **narrator** who stands outside the story.
- In the **first person** as with *Great Expectations,* or
- In the **third person** (he/she)

The voice can have different tones and styles, for example:

- Reflective or wistful ('Time passed and still I waited for her reply. Waited as the seasons passed.')
- Lively and familiar ('I mean, what was I meant to do? Live without my mobile? Give me a break!')
- Harsh and bitter ('The kettle hissed. She stared at it sullenly. Outside a cold rain battered the windows.')

❸ How would you describe the narrator's voice in the extract from *Great Expectations* on page 15? Consider the ideas above as well as any in the box below.

> comical, ironic, angry, thoughtful, regretful, sad, hopeful,   warm, critical

There are different kinds of narrative voice.

1 An **omniscient narrator** has the overview of the story and perhaps knows facts that the characters, or the reader don't know. Consider this example from *The Hound of the Baskervilles* by Sir Arthur Conan Doyle, when the reader is told about the principal character:

> *Mr Sherlock Holmes, who was usually very late in the mornings, save upon those not infrequent occasions when he was up all night, was seated at the breakfast table.*

2 A **self-conscious narrator** reminds the reader that they are reading a work of fiction. For example, the narrator in *Jane Eyre* by Charlotte Brontë addresses the reader directly:

> *Reader, it is not pleasant to dwell on these details. Some say there is enjoyment in looking back to painful experience past; but at this day I can scarcely bear to review the times to which I allude.*

3 A **first person narrator** tells the story from the personal point of view (I) as one of the characters, usually the main one.

4 A point-of-view **third-person narrator** is where the narrative is filtered through a character's point of view (often the protagonist) but in the third person (he/she).

Multiple narrators can also be employed to narrate from the point of view of more than one character, each adding something to the story.

In *Great Expectations*, the story is told by Pip, and whilst it is often vocalised by a young Pip, is framed by his older self. An example of this is when Joe comes to visit Pip in London, and is awkward and ill at ease. The narrative voice tells the reader:

> *I had neither the good sense nor the good feeling to know that this was all my fault, and that if I had been easier with Joe, Joe would have been easier with me.*

EXAM FOCUS

Note how a student has analysed Dickens's use of narrative voice in the above extract from *Great Expectations*:

Comments on the tone of the narrative voice, using direct evidence from the text

In this passage Pip reflects on his character and his actions as a younger man. The older first-person narrator uses two, balanced negative phrases, 'neither the good sense, nor the good feeling', to emphasise his lack of judgement and sensitivity as a young man. The narrative voice is critical, reinforced by the statement 'this was all my fault', which gives the passage a stern and regretful tone.

Identifies the type of narrator

Analyses the structure of the narrator's comment

④ Match the extracts below to two of the different types of narrative voice given above. To help with this, look for:

- The first or third person ('I' or 'he/she')
- How much the narrator appears to know about events

Pride and Prejudice by Jane Austen	'Fake Smile' by Mike Gould
Mr. Bennet was so odd a mixture of quick parts, sarcastic humour, reserve, and caprice, that the experience of three and twenty years had been insufficient to make his wife understand his character. Her mind was less difficult to develop. She was a woman of mean understanding, little information, and uncertain temper.	*Thing is, you can never tell with people. Look at me. Who am I? Ok – I'm a school student. I'm a daughter. But inside are the roots of an old woman. Wise, grey, slow. Am I beautiful? Or plain? Sometimes I feel like a million dollars. Some days I'm not worth a cent.*

APPLYING YOUR SKILLS   (A01) (A02)

⑤ Write a paragraph of 150 words about each of these writers' use of narrative voice. Include comment on:

- The type of narrator
- The style/tone of voice

Make sure you refer to examples from each text.

1.6 LANGUAGE AND STYLE

In both English Language and English Literature GCSEs, you will need to demonstrate a thorough understanding of how language and style creates **mood** and **tone** in writing.

Consider how this has been achieved in the following extract by Mary Shelley from *Frankenstein*, where the creature has just been brought to life:

[1] Powerful nouns create a strong impression of disaster

[3] Ironic repetition of 'beautiful' linked with the exclamation, builds a sense of horror

How can I describe my emotions at this catastrophe, [1] *or how delineate the wretch* [1] *whom with such infinite pains and care I had endeavoured to form?* [2] *His limbs were in proportion and I had selected his features as beautiful. Beautiful! – Great God!* [3] *His yellow skin scarcely covered the work of his muscles and arteries beneath; his hair was of a lustrous black, and flowing; his teeth of a pearly whiteness;* [4] *but these luxuriances only formed a more horrid contrast with his watery eyes.*

[2] Rhetorical question demonstrates the depth of the narrator's despair

[4] Link with the conventional ideas of beauty highlights hideousness of the monster

❶ What do the use of the phrases, 'yellow skin', 'horrid contrast' and 'watery eyes' contribute to the mood and tone?

VOCABULARY

This refers to the word choices made by the writer and their impact. These can include:

Concrete nouns and **adjectives** refer to things we experience and understand through our senses, for example, 'cold', 'fluffy', 'chair'.

Abstract nouns convey an idea, feeling or concept, for example, 'fair', 'helpful', 'unprofessional', mean.

Synonyms are words that are very similar in meaning but still convey subtle differences, for example, synonyms for 'happy' could be 'content', 'jolly', 'untroubled', 'care-free'.

Factual or descriptive – in order to communicate a clear picture to the reader, writers can be very factual, giving us direct information about something, or can describe the effect and feeling generated.

❷ Consider sentences A and B below about a buzzard.
   a) Decide what approach each takes – factual or descriptive?
   b) Find two instances of concrete language in the factual sentence and two instances of abstract language in the descriptive.

A

A buzzard is a large, brown bird of prey that has rounded wing-ends and hunts rabbits and other small animals.

B

The buzzard soared effortlessly on broad, rounded wings, its predatory eye scanning the ground for any sign of movement from the hapless small creatures below.

STYLE

Style can be created in writing by particular vocabulary choices and the tone of the language. Style can also be created through the use of a whole range of literary devices and techniques.

Consider the following stylistic features, which are explored in more detail in 3.5 Imagery and other literary techniques:

Sound effects	Imagery
Repetition – the use of the same or similar words or phrases in close proximity	Personification – the giving of the qualities of a living thing to an inanimate object
Alliteration – the repetition of consonant sounds in close proximity	Simile – the direct comparison of one thing with another
Assonance – the repetition of the same vowel sounds in words in close proximity	Metaphor – an indirect comparison where something is described in terms of something else
Onomatopoeia – words that imitate, when spoken, the sound they describe	Symbol – something concrete used to represent an abstract concept or idea

❸ Read the following and identify two sound effects and one example of imagery. What is the impact of each on the meaning of the sentence?

> *The desert wind screeched across the dunes, scorching as dragon's breath, shrivelling life in all its forms.*

APPLYING YOUR SKILLS   A02 A02

Read the following passage from *The Young King* by Oscar Wilde where, on the night before his coronation, a prince has a disturbing dream. A student has highlighted some of the chosen vocabulary and literary devices that contribute towards the style of the piece.

❹ Make your own notes for highlighted style points 3, 4, 8, 9 and 11.

[1] Past participle suggests the directionless walk in an unfamiliar environment

[5] Offers a highly visual image

[7] Alliteration adds impact to this visual image

And he fell asleep again, and dreamed, and this was his dream.

He thought that he was wandering *[1] through a dim wood,* hung with strange fruits and with beautiful poisonous flowers *[2]. The* adders hissed *[3] at him as he went by, and the* bright parrots flew screaming from branch to branch. *[4]* Huge tortoises lay asleep upon the hot mud. *[5] The trees were full of* apes and peacocks *[6].*

On and on he went, till he reached the outskirts of the wood, and there he saw an immense multitude of men *[7] toiling in the bed of a dried-up river. They* swarmed up the crag like ants. *[8] They dug deep pits in the ground and went down into them. Some of them* cleft *[9] the rocks with great axes; others* grabbled *[10] in the sand.*

They tore up the cactus by its roots, and trampled on the scarlet blossoms. *[11] They hurried about, calling to each other, and no man was idle.*

[2] Vivid details hint at the dangerous nature of the wood

[6] Chooses more exotic details to depict the wood

[10] Uses a highly descriptive verb for this searching movement

1.7 UNDERSTANDING CONTEXT

In English Literature GCSE, you will need to understand what **context** is, and how different elements of it can help you demonstrate a broader understanding of a text.

WHAT IS CONTEXT?

The term 'context' can be linked to a number of different things:

- The time period in which the text was written
- The wider historical context of that period
- The social conditions of the time: class status, housing, health issues
- Political, cultural or religious views and beliefs of the period
- Perception of race, gender or sexuality

HISTORICAL CONTEXT

An example of this type of contextualisation can be seen in the writing of Charles Dickens. Dickens was writing in Victorian London at a time of great social and industrial change which led to the rise of the new middle classes and a developing social conscience about the conditions of the working classes. Although white and middle class, Dickens was concerned about conditions for the poor, a cause he championed during his lifetime.

Read the extract below from *A Christmas Carol* by Charles Dickens. The family of Scrooge's clerk, Bob Cratchit, have just finished their Christmas dinner:

> *Bob Cratchit told them how he had a situation in his eye for Master Peter, which would bring in, if obtained, full five-and-sixpence weekly. The two young Cratchits laughed tremendously at the idea of Peter's being a man of business; and Peter himself looked thoughtfully at the fire from between his collars, as if deliberating what particular investments he should favour when he came into the receipt of that bewildering income. Martha, who was a poor apprentice at a milliner's, then told them what kind of work she had to do, and how many hours she worked at a stretch, and how she meant to lie a-bed tomorrow morning for a good long rest; tomorrow being a holiday she passed at home.*

❶ Identify two aspects of concern for the conditions of the poor that are portrayed in this extract and explain their effect on the reader.

> **TOP TIP**
>
> Ensure that your focus remains with the text and how its context influences it. Avoid getting distracted by the wider history or the writer's biography unless directly relevant to the work.

❷ Write a short paragraph about how the place and time in which it was written are reflected in one of the texts that you have studied.

SOCIAL CONTEXT

Texts can often be set in different periods from the time in which they are written. Shakespeare often wrote about past events.

This is particularly relevant, for example, in *An Inspector Calls* by J. B. Priestley, which is set in 1912, but was published in 1947. Priestley had become interested in politics, social inequality and responsibility and sets this play two years before the start of the First World War, a period of distinct class division, when women were seen as socially inferior to men and working women as a source of cheap labour. The play is about the suicide of a young working woman who falls upon hard times brought about by a series of actions by members of the same middle-class family.

Read the following extract:

> INSPECTOR: There are a lot of young women living that sort of existence in every city and big town in this country, Miss Birling. If there weren't, the factories and warehouses wouldn't know where to look for cheap labour. Ask your father.
>
> SHEILA: But these girl's aren't cheap labour – they're *people*.
>
> INSPECTOR (*dryly*): I've had that notion myself from time to time. In fact, I've thought that it would do us all a bit of good if sometimes we tried to put ourselves in the place of these young women counting their pennies in their dingy little back bed-rooms.
>
> SHEILA: Yes, I expect it would.

❸ How does Sheila's reaction to the Inspector's comments reflect the context in which the play is set?

AIMING HIGH ⭐

Your starting point should always be the text when exploring context. Focus on small details about setting (for example, a landscape or the furnishings of a room) or a character's appearance (clothing, manner, etc.) to make wider thematic points about class or values. For example, Priestley's description of the Birling house as 'fairly large ... but not cosy or homelike' could link to the attitudes of middle-class businessmen of the period, like Mr Birling.

CULTURAL CONTEXT

There is also the wider context of how the text you are studying links with similar types of genres. For example, *An Inspector Calls* was written after a time in which many plays – such as *The Importance of Being Ernest* by Oscar Wilde, featured middle or upper class people in slightly ridiculous romantic situations. However, there is nothing comic or even very romantic about *An Inspector Calls.* Instead it might be seen as playing with audience's expectations of a drawing-room drama and stirring their social conscience.

Similarly, through context, you can look at how different works of literature approach typical romantic scenes – such as ones in which a proposal of marriage is made.

EXAM FOCUS

Consider the following extract from *Pride and Prejudice* by Jane Austen in which Elizabeth Bennet is receiving a proposal of marriage from Mr Darcy that she is about to decline. A student has begun some annotations on the attitudes Elizabeth displays.

> Expresses Elizabeth's personal feelings

> Knows her mind but shows pity expected of her

In spite of her deeply-rooted dislike, she could not be insensible to the compliments of such a man's affection, and though her intentions did not vary for an instant, she was at first sorry for the pain he was to receive; still, roused to resentment by his subsequent language, she lost all compassion in anger. She tried, however, to compose herself to answer him with patience, when he should have done. He concluded with representing to her the strength of that attachment, which in spite of all his endeavours, he had found impossible to conquer... As he said this, she could easily see that he had no doubt at all of a favourable answer... Such a circumstance could only exasperate further and when he ceased, the colour in her cheeks rose...

> Shows she know how she should behave when receiving a proposal

❹   Select further words or phrases from the extract that suggest how:

   a) a female character traditionally might have responded in this situation

   b) Elizabeth actually wants to respond

APPLYING YOUR SKILLS

Read the following extract from *Pigeon English* by Stephen Kelman. It is from the beginning of the book where Harrison, the boy telling the story, has just finished speaking to his father who is still in Ghana. Harrison, together with his mother and sister, are newly arrived in Britain.

> *Papa's voice was smiling. I love it when his voice is smiling, it means you did good. I didn't need to washing my hands after, my pigeon doesn't have any germs. They're always telling you to wash your hands. Asweh, there's so many germs here you wouldn't believe it! Everybody's scared of them all the time. Germs from Africa are the most deadliest, that's why Vilis ran away when I tried to say hello to him, he thinks if he breathes my germs he'll die.*
>
> *I didn't even know I brought the germs with me. You can't feel or see them or anything. Adjei, germs are very tricky! I don't even care if Vilis hates me, he's a dirty tackler and he never passes the ball to me.*

⑤ How does the writer convey Harrison's social and cultural background in this passage? Think about:
- How he speaks about his father
- What he says about Vilis and his treatment of him?

PROGRESS CHECK FOR CHAPTER ONE

GOOD PROGRESS

I can:
- Read critically with a good understanding of genre and form, and how the purpose of communicating a core idea and themes to a particular audience, can be achieved ☐
- Understand how facts, statistics and opinions can be used to particular effect in writing ☐
- Understand how character, voice, language, style and context inform a text's meaning ☐

EXCELLENT PROGRESS

I can:
- Reflect critically and evaluating the impact of genre and form, identifying a range of themes and analysing the effectiveness of their impact on their intended audience ☐
- Analyse texts in a detailed way, exploring the effectiveness of using facts, statistics and opinions ☐
- Demonstrate a wide-ranging knowledge of writers' skills, including thoughtful analysis of context ☐

2.1 USING QUOTATIONS AND EVIDENCE

In both English Language and English Literature GCSEs you will need to be able to read carefully and with understanding, selecting the right type of information when asked to do so and supporting your ideas by referring closely to the texts.

There are a number of different ways in which this can be done.

DIRECT QUOTATIONS

When you reproduce a specific part of the text to illustrate a point this is quoting directly. To do this effectively you should:

● Choose the best possible **quotation** to illustrate your point
● Keep quotations as short as possible. Once you've identified the section you want to use, try and select the best words, phrase or sentence to illustrate your point
● Use quotation marks ('…') to separate the quoted text from your own words
● Quote the words directly as written
● Make your quotations flow as part of your writing – embed them within your sentences
● If you want to use an extract, but to miss out a section for brevity, you can indicate there is a missing part by the use of square brackets containing **ellipses** [...]
● Give a reference for your quotation. Extracts supplied in the exam will have line numbers so use these to indicate where your quotation has come from
● If you are quoting from memory, add a chapter or section reference in brackets

Read the following extract from Daphne du Maurier's *Rebecca*. It is from the beginning when the young second wife first arrives at her husband's house. It is where he used to live with his first wife.

> *Suddenly I saw a clearing in the dark drive ahead, and a patch of sky, and in a moment the dark trees had thinned, the nameless shrubs had disappeared, and on either side of us was a wall of colour, blood-red, reaching far above our heads. We were amongst the*
> 5 *rhododendrons. There was something bewildering, even shocking, about the suddenness of their discovery. The woods had not prepared me for them. They startled me with their crimson faces, massed one upon the other in incredible profusion, showing no leaf, no twig, nothing but the slaughterous red, luscious and fantastic, unlike any rhododendron plant I had ever seen before.*

❶ Identify two quotations to support the view that there are ominous, threatening, symbolic elements to the appearance of the rhododendrons.

❷   Now, write a paragraph which explains the appearance of the flowers and includes quotations to support the points made.

❸   Finally, compare and evaluate your examples with those given below. Which is yours closest to?

Answer	Particular features
Lower level use of quotation	
The description of the rhododendrons is rather threatening. Their crimson faces massed one upon the other in incredible profusion showing no leaf no twig nothing but the slaughterous red luscious and fantastic unlike any rhododendron plant I had ever seen before.	• Example is too long – better if individual words such as 'startled', 'slaughterous' and 'fantastic' were quoted and the impact explained • No line references • No quotation marks included • Commas have been omitted • Very limited explanation of the quotation
Good level use of quotation	
The description of the rhododendrons is rather threatening with the colour described as 'blood-red' in line three, and with the unusual adjective 'slaughterous' in line seven, suggesting death. The colour red is also a **symbol** of both love and danger, which is again, an ominous indication for the future of the young bride.	• Short quotations used and the impact of the word choices explained • Quotations are accurate and marked by quotation marks • Line references included • Quotations are seamlessly included in the answer and meaning is elaborated further

In the good level response above, there are additional opportunities to comment on the symbolism of the colour red.

❹   a) Find two further quotations that indicate Rebecca's reaction to the rhododendrons and put them into sentences.

   b) How might her reaction to them contribute to the tense atmosphere around this first visit to her new home?

EVIDENCING

Sometimes it can be more efficient to **paraphrase** rather than use long quotations. Paraphrasing means putting the meaning or ideas of something into your own words.

In order to paraphrase, you need to do the following:

- Understand the overall meaning – the 'gist'
- Put that meaning in your own words succinctly, without using the same language as the original text

To do this, using **synonyms** can be very useful. For example, the word 'fume' is similar to 'fog', 'mist', 'cloud', 'smoke'. Used metaphorically it could refer to 'confusion', 'blindness', 'vagueness' etc.

⑤ a) What words could replace 'hard' in the phrase 'hard journey'?

b) In the list below, find a suitable synonym for 'warder' in the phrase 'warder of the brain'

> guard   custodian   officer   servant
> gate-keeper   jailer

In Shakespeare's *Macbeth*, Lady Macbeth outlines the following plan to murder King Duncan:

> *When Duncan is asleep,*
> *Whereto the rather shall his day's hard journey* [1]
> *Soundly invite him, his two chamberlains*
> *Will I with wine* [2] *and wassail so convince*
> *That memory, the warder of the brain,*
> *Shall be a fume,* [3] *and the receipt of reason*
> *A limbeck only. When in swinish sleep*
> *Their drenched natures lies as in a death,* [4]
> *What cannot you and I perform upon*
> *Th' unguarded Duncan?* [5] *What not put upon*
> *His spongy officers, who shall bear the guilt* [6]
> *Of our great quell?*   1:7:60-72

The above speech, from Lady Macbeth, could therefore be paraphrased as follows:

> Lady Macbeth's plan is to wait until Duncan is fast asleep after his tiring journey [1] and then get his guards drunk [2] until they are in an alcoholic stupor [3]. She and Macbeth will then be able to murder Duncan [5] and blame the guards. [6]

The numbers show how the core information has been transferred from the source text to the explanation above.

⑥ Paraphrase the following passage in no more than 30 words:

> School dinners, from my childhood, were a thing of dread: mashed potato with grey lumps, cheap, gristly meat, and cabbage boiled to obliteration. Even the puddings were grim. There were chocolate puddings with no trace of chocolate and dreadful concoctions with tapioca, affectionately known by us as 'frogspawn'. Worst of all, you were expected to eat it all.

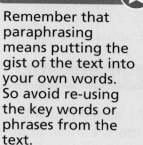

TOP TIP

Remember that paraphrasing means putting the gist of the text into your own words. So avoid re-using the key words or phrases from the text.

APPLYING YOUR SKILLS   (A01)

⑦ Read this extract from *Jane Eyre* by Charlotte Brontë. Then, write about how Jane feels about Mr Rochester and Thornfield. Make sure you:

   a) Include one direct quotation that shows what Jane says to Rochester (be careful – not the words in speech marks)

   b) Paraphrase her range of physical reactions. You could start in this way:

   Jane feels strongly about Thornfield. This is shown by…

> In listening, I sobbed convulsively; for I could repress what I endured no longer; I was obliged to yield, and I was shaken from head to foot with acute distress. When I did speak, it was only to express an impetuous wish that I had never been born, or never come to Thornfield.
>
> 'Because you are sorry to leave it?'
>
> The vehemence of emotion, stirred by grief and love within me, was claiming mastery, and struggled for full sway; and asserting a right to predominate: to overcome, to live, rise and reign at last; yes, – and to speak.

2.2 IDENTIFYING EXPLICIT AND IMPLICIT INFORMATION

One of the things that you will be expected to be able to do, particularly in English Language GCSE, is to extract information from a text.

EXPLICIT INFORMATION

An **explicit** meaning is one that is stated clearly, and allows little room for interpretation or doubt. Consider the following extract from *The Diary of a Nobody* by George and Weedon Grossmith:

> *Carrie and I can manage to pass our evenings together without friends. There is always something to be done: a tin-tack here, a Venetian blind to put straight, a fan to nail up, or part of a carpet to nail down – all of which I can do with my pipe in my mouth; while Carrie is not above putting a button on a shirt, mending a pillow-case, or practising the 'Sylvia Gavotte' on our new cottage piano (on the three years' system), manufactured by W. Bilkson (in small letter), from Collard and Collard (in very large letters). It is also a great comfort to us to know that our boy Willie is getting on so well in the Bank at Oldham. We should like to see more of him.*

Explicit information about Carrie and the narrator would include the following:

- Both the narrator and his partner can do small jobs around the home
- They have a piano which Carrie plays
- They have a son who works at a bank in Oldham

❶ What information are we told explicitly about the piano?

IMPLICIT INFORMATION

An **implicit** meaning is something indirectly stated, suggested or hinted at. Writers embed implied meanings to draw the reader in and to create depth of meaning in their texts. For example:

> *He stared at his grey desk. The pile of grey folders. The grey box-like laptop. He sighed.*

The implied meaning here is that: the man hates his job. We can work out or **infer** this from:

- The repetition of the dull colours
- The verbs 'stared' and 'sighed'

❷ Now re-read the extract from *Diary of a Nobody* above up to 'pipe in my mouth', and think about what this section suggests in terms of the couple's relationship.

Other implicit information in the above passage may include the following:

- The suggestion that Carrie 'is not above' doing her own mending suggests they are lower middle class, using servants for some things but probably not being able to afford them for others
- The fact that they have a piano, albeit a small one purchased on credit, suggests that they aspire to move up the social scale
- The reference to the lettering on the piano suggests that the narrator is rather particular about details and is also concerned about branding and appearing to own the right thing

❸ What do the final two sentences imply about the couple's relationship with their son?

TOP TIP

Don't be tempted to make wild guesses at what is meant from one word. Implicit information or ideas often become clear once you analyse several 'clues'.

APPLYING YOUR SKILLS

Read the following extract about British coastal areas:

> The coastal areas of the United Kingdom vary greatly. There are the tired facades of the historic resorts beloved of our Victorian ancestors now reduced to 'kiss me quick' hats, sticks of rock in gaudy colours suggestive of E numbers, and brine beleaguered pitch- and- putt. These are in stark contrast to the intimate coves and craggy shorelines of Devon and Cornwall, the endless beaches, castellated cliff tops and big skies of Northumbria or the windswept, bleak beauty of the Scottish Islands. Britain is a country of diverse landscapes and nowhere is this better reflected than in our coastal landscapes.

❹ Summarise, in one sentence, what we are told explicitly about the coastal areas of Britain in this text.

❺ What is suggested implicitly about the narrator's view of the historic resorts? What makes you think this?

2.3 INTERPRETING INFORMATION

One of the skills required for both English Language and English Literature GCSEs is the ability to interpret information provided by texts and make your own judgments on character and viewpoint, supported by evidence.

WEIGHING UP INTERPRETATIONS

Consider the information offered in this extract from *A Christmas Carol* by Charles Dickens. Scrooge is being taken, by the Spirit of Christmas present, to visit unseen the Christmas celebrations of his clerk, Bob Cratchit and his family.

> *'It should be Christmas Day, I am sure,' said she, 'on which one drinks the health of such an odious, stingy, hard, unfeeling man as Mr Scrooge. You know he is, Robert! Nobody knows it better than you do, poor fellow!'*
>
> 5   *'My dear,' was Bob's mild answer, 'Christmas Day.'*
>
> *'I'll drink his health for your sake and the Day's', said Mrs Cratchit, 'not for his. Long life to him! A merry Christmas and a happy new year! – he'll be very merry and very happy, I have no doubt!'*
>
> *The children drank the toast after her. It was the first of their proceedings which had no heartiness in it.*

It tells the reader the following:

1. Mrs Cratchit doesn't like Scrooge.
2. Mrs Cratchit thinks Scrooge is mean and unsympathetic.
3. She only raises a toast to him because of her husband and because it is Christmas.

However, there is more that can be gleaned from the text by interpreting the information further.

❶   Locate the following in the first three lines of the extract above:
   ● The listing of strong adjectives suggesting the depth of Mrs Cratchit's dislike of Scrooge
   ● Her view that Bob doesn't openly acknowledge Scrooge's failings
   ● The implication that Bob is particularly affected by Scrooge, but is also very forgiving of him

❷   Further information can be obtained about Scrooge by interpreting lines 5–9 of the extract. Answer these questions:
   a) For whose sake does Mrs Cratchit make the toast?
   b) How does she think Scrooge feels about Christmas and what does this say about him?
   c) What is the Cratchit children's view of Scrooge and why might this be?

❸ What overall interpretation do you think is supported by the points in question 2?

   a) That Mrs Cratchit is not a very kind or forgiving woman

   b) That Mrs Cratchit is kind but Scrooge's treatment of Bob pushes her too far

   c) That Mrs Cratchit only cares about her own family not anyone else?

TOP TIP

You can also interpret a character by considering how *unlike* another character they are from the same text. Drawing contrasts in this way can open up interesting ideas.

Scrooge's character is revealed in the extract on page 30 by how others react to him. However, the reader can also find out about a character through the narrative voice and from what he does and says himself.

Consider the following extract which precedes the above scene at the Cratchits', on Christmas Eve:

> *At length the hour of shutting up the counting-house arrived. With an ill-will Scrooge dismounted from his stool, and tacitly admitted the fact to the expectant clerk in the tank, who instantly snuffed his candle out, and put on his hat.*
> 5   *'You'll want all day tomorrow, I suppose?' said Scrooge.*
>   *'If quite convenient, sir.'*
> *'It's not convenient,' said Scrooge, 'and it's not fair. If I was to stop half-a-crown for it, you'd think yourself ill used, I'll be bound.'*

❹ What do the following actions and speech imply about Scrooge?

	Action or speech	Implication
A	'With an ill-will Scrooge dismounted from his stool'	The fact that he gets down with an 'ill-will' suggests he has something unpleasant in mind.
B	'the expectant clerk in the tank, who instantly snuffed his candle out, and put on his hat'	
C	'You'll want all day tomorrow, I suppose?' said Scrooge'	
D	'If I was to stop half-a-crown for it, you'd think yourself ill used, I'll be bound'	

APPLYING YOUR SKILLS   (A01) (A02)

❺ Choose a significant character from a text you have studied and select one main characteristic. Find an example of how the writer demonstrates this characteristic through each of the following:

   ● What the narrative voice says about that character

   ● What the character does and says themselves

   ● What others say about the character and how they respond to them

2.4 SUMMARISING AND SYNTHESISING INFORMATION

In English Language GCSE, you will be required to read and take in key information quickly, processing the main points for comparison. In English Literature GCSE, you will be comparing the ideas in two poems or linking ideas in an extract with those in the text as a whole.

SUMMARY

You must be able to summarise main points, or the 'what' of a text, in a clear, concise way to show your understanding. Read the following extract:

> *He'd never wanted a dog in the first place. He considered them to be noisy, unhygienic creatures, stuck in the state of a perpetual toddler, attention-seeking and, quite frankly, a bit smelly. He hadn't been brought up with animals and he had no intention of changing that status in adulthood.*
>
> *It took his seven-year-old daughter all of three months to persuade him. She used every trick in her arsenal. She cajoled, pleaded, sulked and cried bitter tears. She looked longingly after every dog she met, no matter how flea-bitten and aged, and eventually he could resist no longer. Tortured by the unrequited longing of his young off-spring, he capitulated and bought her a puppy.*
>
> *Unfortunately, they inadvertently chose the naughtiest dog in the world.*

Summarising involves identifying the main points about something and writing them in as few words as possible. For example, if you were asked about the father, you would look for reference to 'father' or 'he' and anything he does, says or feels such as:

- Didn't want a dog
- Found them noisy, dirty and demanding
- Hadn't been brought up with dogs
- Persuaded to get a dog by his daughter

❶ Now locate the main points in the extract about the following:

   a) the daughter

   b) the dog

SYNTHESIS

Synthesis is when you bring together several points from a text or between two texts to comment on or explain ideas. To do this you need to:

- Be clear about the points you are bringing together
- Write about them in succinct, clear sentences, using **connectives** such as 'in the same way' or 'however'

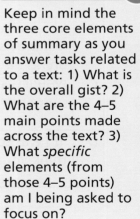

AIMING HIGH ★

Keep in mind the three core elements of summary as you answer tasks related to a text: 1) What is the overall gist? 2) What are the 4–5 main points made across the text? 3) What *specific* elements (from those 4–5 points) am I being asked to focus on?

TOP TIP ★

Make two lists of connectives; one that suggests what may be different and one suggesting what is similar. Keep them ready to use when you are writing about two or more texts.

Read this second extract about a different experience of a father acquiring a dog for his son:

> I'd always wanted to get a family dog. I'd had dogs as a child myself and knew the benefit of their companionship, loyalty and unconditional love. They also teach children about caring and taking responsibility for another living creature. So, as soon as my son started to express an interest, we researched carefully and Alfie came into our lives.

❷ Summarise two reasons why the father in the second passage felt getting a dog was a good idea.

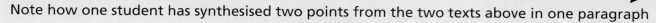

EXAM FOCUS

Note how one student has synthesised two points from the two texts above in one paragraph

> In the first text the father is very reluctant to get a dog whereas in the second, he is keen.

❸ Continue the paragraph, synthesising further points from the two extracts about getting a dog.

APPLYING YOUR SKILLS

(A02)

Consider the following poem 'Spellbound' by Emily Brontë.

> The night is darkening round me,
> The wild winds coldly blow;
> But a tyrant spell has bound me
> And I cannot, cannot go.
>
> 5 The giant trees are bending
> Their bare boughs weighed with snow.
> And the storm is fast descending
> And yet I cannot go.
>
> Clouds beyond clouds above me,
> 10 Wastes beyond wastes below;
> But nothing drear can move me;
> I will not, cannot go.

❹ How would you summarise the environment and the relationship between the poetic voice and the surroundings?
- Look for words relating to the time of day, weather and scenery
- Identify words that explain the effect of the surroundings on the person

PROGRESS CHECK FOR CHAPTER TWO

GOOD PROGRESS

I can:
- Select main points and summarise them ☐
- Synthesise points from different texts into a short comparison ☐

EXCELLENT PROGRESS

I can:
- Summarise main points concisely and succinctly ☐
- Synthesise points effectively and comparatively from two texts ☐

3.1 WRITERS' METHODS AND EFFECTS

Writers' methods – the techniques authors employ – are a vital element of both English Language and English Literature study. You will need to comment critically on such methods and analyse the effects they create.

COMMENTING ON WRITERS' METHODS

Writers' methods are the techniques writers use – the 'how' of writing.

Consider the following extract from *Jane Eyre* by Charlotte Brontë in which Jane speaks to Rochester:

> *'Do you think, because I am poor, obscure, plain, and little, I am soulless and heartless? You think wrong! – I have as much soul as you, – and full as much heart! And if God had gifted me with some beauty, and much wealth, I should have made it as hard for you to*
> 5 *leave me, as it is now for me to leave you. I am not talking to you now through the medium of custom, conventionalities, or even of mortal flesh: – it is my spirit that addresses your spirit; just as if both had passed through the grave, and we stood at God's feet, equal, – as we are!'*

Some of the methods used here to communicate the writer's view on women's position in society include:

- Narrative view – written from Jane's perspective
- Character and voice – Jane addresses Rochester strongly and directly
- Language and style – effective simple language and short adjectives, 'poor, obscure, plain, and little'. Also uses vocabulary from a specific **semantic field** such as 'soul', 'heart' and 'spirit'. Literary techniques – listing in the first line, are combined with the **assonance** of the 'o' sound and the **alliteration** of 'God' and 'gifted' in line 3, and 'custom' and 'conventionalities' in line 6.

❶ Identify the different uses and styles of:

   a) Punctuation

   b) Sentences

TOP TIP

Note that in GCSE English Literature, AO2 is solely dedicated to writers' methods and effects, indicating their importance.

ANALYSING EFFECTS

Effects are the result of the writer's methods – their impact on the reader.

Consider the effect of the different methods employed in the extract.

- Narrative view – Jane's perspective makes the reader identify and sympathise with Jane
- Character and voice – the effect is to make Jane seem a brave and determined voice
- Language and style – Jane's strong speech, comparing her situation with Rochester's emphasises their common humanity against a backdrop of social inequality

❷ Now explain the effects of these methods:

a) Punctuation – what mood is created by Brontë's use of question marks, **dashes**, exclamations?

b) Structure – what effect is created by the mixture of sentences styles you noted earlier? What effect do the **rhetorical questions** have? What is Brontë attempting to show in the longer sentences?

c) Literary techniques – what is the effect of the alliteration and assonance?

❸ Bearing all these things in mind, what overall impression is given of Jane from this passage? Write at least one paragraph. You could start:

Brontë presents Jane as someone who …

APPLYING YOUR SKILLS (A02)(A02)

Read the following passage from *The Yellow Wallpaper* by Charlotte Perkins Gilman about a woman suffering from mental illness.

> *This bed will not move!*
>
> *I tried to lift and push it until I was lame, and then I got so angry I bit off a little piece at one corner – but it hurt my teeth.*
>
> *Then I peeled off all the paper I could reach standing on the floor. It sticks horribly and the pattern just enjoys it! All those strangled heads and bulbous eyes and waddling fungus growths just shriek with derision!*
>
> *I am getting angry enough to do something desperate. To jump out of the window would be admirable exercise, but the bars are too strong even to try.*
>
> *Besides I wouldn't do it. Of course not. I know well enough that a step like that is improper and might be misconstrued.*

❹ a) Create a table like the one below giving examples of the different methods used here by Perkins Gilman, and their effects.

Writer's method	Examples from The Yellow Wallpaper	Effect on reader
Narrative view	First person – direct account of events	
Character and voice		
Language and style	Starts with a short exclamatory sentence	
Structure		
Literary techniques		
Punctuation		

b) Select one or two of the methods used with examples and write about their effects in explanatory sentences. You should write between 50–75 words.

3.2 VOCABULARY FOR EFFECT

One of the fundamental requirements for both English Language and English Literature GCSE is that you can analyse and explain how writers use particular words and phrases to achieve effects and influence their readers.

VOCABULARY CHOICES

Words are at the heart of the craft of writing and a writer's choice of vocabulary represents a significant decision in creating the intended meaning. Here are some factors that influence these choices:

- **Weak/powerful words**: selecting the strength of impact the chosen word will have. Look at the following adjective pairings. Both words mean roughly the same but one is weak and the other powerful.

sad/distraught		angry/furious		good/angelic

hot/boiling		painful/excruciating

❶ Note down three more adjective pairings like this that are weaker and stronger expressions of the same emotion or quality.

- **Formal/informal vocabulary** – the way in which a character's words convey their thoughts, actions and speech, can give a very different impression.

  Consider the following two messages left on an answerphone:

AIMING HIGH

Look out for the semantic field (or fields) in a text. These are sets of closely related words which are linked by subject matter or grammatical use and can build a vivid picture or accurate account. For example, a text about a landscape might use lots of similar noun phrases related to flooding: 'overflowing ditches', 'battered sandbags', 'creaking dams' and 'bursting storm-drains'.

A

Hello. Thank you for helping me out yesterday. It had been raining heavily so I was disappointed when the bus didn't arrive. It was good of you, as a colleague I hardly know, to stop and offer me a lift.

B

Hi there! Cheers for helping me out yesterday. It'd been bucketing down so I was gutted when the bus didn't arrive. It was cool of you, as my workmate who I hardly know, to stop and offer me a lift.

❷ Which message is more informal and 'friendly'? What difference in vocabulary choices do you notice?

- **Technical vocabulary** implies a greater knowledge in the reader, for example: 'A cacophony arose from the corvids' implies an understanding not suggested by the less technical 'The crows were noisy'.

③ What specialist or technical vocabulary can you identify in the following extract? What does it suggest about the woman?

> She swiftly removed the fixed focus lens from the camera's body and attached the telephoto, then set the focal length. Just in time: the lions were coming out of their enclosure...

- **Combining words** can create several different effects, for example, **adjectives** use with **intensifiers** (often adverbs), such as 'totally unbelievable,' add emphasis or strength to an idea or comment.
- **Emotive/objective vocabulary** generates an emotional response in the reader whereas objective vocabulary is factual and observable. Consider the difference between the phrases 'wrenched from the heart of his family' and 'taken into care', for example.

④ What words or phrases create a powerful or emotional effect in the following paragraph?

> The lions looked utterly bored. How they must have longed for the freedom of the plains! She felt thoroughly miserable, and put her camera away.

TOP TIP

One of the ways you can evaluate the effect of a particular word choice is to try substituting it with another as this can reveal the particular impact of a specific word choice.

Read the following passage from *Pigeon English* by Stephen Kelman, written from the point of view of a young boy, Harrison, describing a neighbour and his dog.

Consider the effect of particular words highlighted by the annotations.

Shortened version of 'I swear' which indicates Harrison's **accent** and ethnicity

The correct version of this English **idiom** would be 'donkey's years'. Kelman shows that Harrison is starting to assimilate the language by attempting to use this expression

> Did you know that dogs can sneeze? Asweh, it's true. I saw it with my own two eyes. Asbo did a big sneeze. It was a shock at first. Nobody suspected it. He did about a
> 5   hundred sneezes. He couldn't stop after the first one, it was like a machine gun. Every sneeze made a new sneeze. Even Asbo was surprised. He couldn't stop for donkey hours.
>   Terry Takeaway: 'He's allergic to beer
> 10 innit.'
>   Terry Takeaway put some beer in his hand and gave it to Asbo to drink but Asbo wouldn't drink it. He just made a sad face and turned his head away and that's when he started sneezing. The bubbles went up his nose.
>   He's called Terry Takeaway because he always takes things away. It's just another name for a thiefman.

An abbreviation for 'anti-social behaviour order', suggests the nature of the environment Terry and Harrison are living in

An unusual choice which may reflect a word in Harrison's own first language

⑤ What does the word 'innit' in line 10 imply about Terry's way of speaking?

⑥ Overall, taking into account the annotations, what impression do you gain of Harrison from his choice of vocabulary?

EXAM FOCUS

Read the following nonfiction passage on increased security in schools and consider what suggested alternative word choices for the first two underlined words, reveal about the original word choices.

[1] a strong word choice suggesting that security levels are absurd. Substituting a more measured word, such as 'high' would suggest a rigorous rather than extreme level.

> Security in some schools has been increased to a ridiculous [1] level. At our local school three metre high metal fencing incarcerates [2] the occupants, whilst surveillance cameras train an unrelenting [3] eye on vulnerable [4] access points. There is a finger-print entry system that denies access randomly to those who are legitimately entitled [5] to enter, whilst allowing those with nimble feet, to follow closely behind when the gate eventually opens to let someone through. It also has a nervous-breakdown [6] when it rains, the wind blows or there's a letter 'r' in the month!

[2] an example of emotive language. Replacing it with a more neutral word such as 'confines' would highlight the negative connotations of the original word choice.

❼ Try using this technique yourself on the four remaining pieces of vocabulary highlighted in the extract.

APPLYING YOUR SKILLS

The Charge of the Light Brigade by Alfred Lord Tennyson, is a poem about a futile cavalry attack in the Crimean War, resulting in heavy casualties and criticism of those in charge. It was written soon after the event, when public emotion was running high, but was later amended with some of the original comment toned down.

❽ a) Consider the extracts from two versions: the original version and the later version. A student has commented on the first pair of quotations, identifying what effect vocabulary choices have made on the meaning. Copy the second row of the table and add your thoughts on the effect of the vocabulary changes here.

Original version	Later version	Effect of change
Came from the jaws of Death	Came through the jaws of Death	The idea of the soldiers coming 'from' the 'jaws of Death' links the soldiers with death itself, whereas the soldiers 'coming through' in the later version is more positive and as though they are escaping death.
Plunged in the battery-smoke With many a desperate stroke The Russian line they broke	Plunged in the battery-smoke Right thro' the line they broke;	

b) Now write 75–100 words on the effects made by the changes you noted in the second pair of quotations.

3.3 SENTENCES FOR IMPACT AND MEANING

It is important for both English Language and English Literature GCSEs that you can explain and analyse how writers use a variety of different sentence types for impact and to create meaning.

SENTENCE TYPES

Type	Definition	Example
Simple sentences	These have one main clause consisting of subject and a verb.	*The bus arrived.* subject verb
Compound sentences	These express two equally important ideas by joining two equal clauses using the **conjunctions** 'and', 'or' 'but' or 'so'.	*I sat down obediently and I drank my tea.* clause 1 conjunction clause 2
Complex sentences	These communicate more than one idea through a main **clause** and one or more **subordinate clauses**, linked by conjunctions.	*Although he felt so elated, he still managed to keep a straight face.* **conjunction sub clause main clause**

Complex sentences provide the opportunity to add extra information and to modify the main idea.

Consider the types of sentences used below in this extract from *Jamacia Inn* by Daphne Du Maurier.

Simple sentence providing a structural finality that reinforces the meaning of the words: events have reached an abrupt conclusion

Compound sentence linking of two ideas with equal weight to suggest the togetherness of the two women in facing their situation

There was no argument after that. Mary would lie herself into hell rather than let her aunt suffer. The situation must be faced though, however ironical her position was to be.

  'Come with me to the door,' she said; 'we'll not keep Mr Bassat long. You needn't be afraid of me; I shall say nothing.'

  They went into the hall together, and Mary unbolted the heavy entrance-door.

Complex sentence emphasising the first part: there is no avoiding the situation

Short sentences tend to speed the pace of writing. Sometimes a short sentence can be used within a passage of longer sentences to give the content particular impact.

Consider the following from *The Hound of the Baskervilles* by Sir Arthur Conan Doyle:

> *But now from somewhere among the broken ground immediately in front of us there came one last despairing yell, and then a dull, heavy thud. We halted and listened. Not another sound broke the heavy silence of the windless night.*

❶ How is the reader affected by the use of this short sentence, 'We halted and listened'? Think about:

    a) What it adds to the pace and the mood of the story

    b) How it contrasts with the use of longer sentences around it

TOP TIP

If there is something significant about the use of different sentence types, identify it and explain what the impact is in terms of the effect on meaning.

QUESTIONS

Sometimes writers use questions for particular purposes in their writing. Often, these are **rhetorical questions** to which an answer is not expected.

❷ What is the added effect of using a question rather than a statement in the examples below?

TOP TIP

If a writer has used rhetorical questions, comment specifically, explaining what their effects are.

Question	Statement
What was I supposed to do?	I didn't know what to do.
Are you just going to stand back and let this happen?	Doing nothing is not an option.

APPLYING YOUR SKILLS

Read the following passage about pet dogs not being kept under proper control:

> *One minute I was walking my dog sedately across the playing field, and the next, two bull terriers were tearing across the grass. Their intentions were not peaceable. One dog immediately started to attack mine, who stood his ground momentarily and then fled. Both Bull Terriers rounded on him in a pincer movement. What was I going to do? Remembering something I'd read, I chose the dominant dog and ran at him screaming like a banshee. I thrust my large golfing umbrella towards his face and opened it suddenly. It worked! He stopped in his tracks, gave me a long look as if considering whether to turn his attentions to me, then thought better of it and finally heeded the previously futile calls of his owner, with the second dog following. I don't know who was shaking more, me or my dog.*

❸ Write a paragraph about the use of sentences to create tension in this passage. The colour coding should help you to identify the simple, compound and complex sentences.

3.4 PARAGRAPHS AND ORGANISATION

In both English Language and English Literature GCSEs you will need to be able to analyse and comment on how writers use paragraphs to create meaning and effects.

PARAGRAPH FUNCTIONS

A **paragraph** is usually a series of sentences that have a common theme or topic, marked by starting a new line. A new paragraph is begun to:

- Introduce a **new or related subject** or a **contrasting point** or **idea**
- Introduce a **new character** or **viewpoint**
- Change the **time** (**flashforwards** or **flashback**) or **location** (from inside to outside or from one place to an entirely different one)
- Change the **mood**, **pace** or **tone** (often as a result of the above)

❶ Read the following passage and identify why, from the reasons listed above, a new paragraph has been started.

> *I stood outside the restaurant, stuck in an agony of indecision. Could I summon the courage to go inside and risk the embarrassment of yet another failed date? Could I remember all the questions I'd prepared in case my mind went blank? I hoped this time it would be different, but now I was actually waiting outside, my resolve was wavering.*
>
> *It had all seemed straightforward when I filled out the online dating form, on my computer, a few months earlier. I had chosen a nice picture from my holidays last year and described all my interests and hobbies, and even my cat!*

Paragraph order is a significant structural feature when analysing a text. You may wish to consider:

- The effect and impact of the order on how meaning is conveyed
- The order in terms of the timeframe or chronology and the effect of any changes to this

❷ Look again at the two paragraphs above. What would be the effect of reversing their order?

Paragraph length varies. Some paragraphs are only a sentence long, some are much longer and this can also affect meaning.

Read the following extract:

> *There was nothing particularly special about that day, initially. I was just walking along with my books in a bag and my laptop stuffed into my rucksack like usual. I had forgotten to go to the cash point and the bus driver was always grumpy if you gave him a tenner for the bus fare, so I was on foot. The sun was shining and life didn't seem too bad.*
>
> *Then I saw him and time stopped, freeze-framed, in an instant.*
>
> *Looking back on it now, I can't believe that we ever met like that, just walking along the same road at the same time. What were the chances of that happening...*

❸ What is the effect of having the short middle paragraph here?

FUNCTIONS OF SENTENCES WITHIN PARAGRAPHS

The **ordering** of sentences within paragraphs also influences the meaning. For example in the following paragraph:

> *The pigeon was gone. One minute it had been part of a flock, pecking discarded crumbs from the platform edge, the next minute, in a flurry of feathers, it had disappeared. It was so fast that the passengers waiting for the 7.15 to Charing Cross barely noticed. If they'd have looked up, tracing the feathers floating gently on the currents of air, back to their source, they would have seen him, stripped plumage and predatory yellow eyes out of place in that most urban of environments. The Sparrow Hawk had just consumed his breakfast.*

❹ What is the paragraph about?

❺ Now look at the second version below. What differences are there and what is the effect of these?

> *The Sparrow Hawk had just consumed his breakfast. If they'd have looked up, tracing the feathers floating gently on the currents of air, back to their source, they would have seen him, stripped plumage and predatory yellow eyes out of place in that most urban of environments. The pigeon was gone. One minute it had been part of a flock, pecking discarded crumbs from the platform edge, the next minute, in a flurry of feathers, it had disappeared. It was so fast that the passengers waiting for the 7.15 to Charing Cross barely noticed.*

TOP TIP

When reading texts analytically, look for changes in the pattern of the writing. If you meet a short paragraph, identify why it has been used and how it impacts on the text's effectiveness.

Read the paragraph below from Stephen Kelman's *Pigeon English*. This comes from the pivotal moment in the plot, when Harrison is stabbed.

> *I didn't see him. He came out of nowhere. He was waiting for me. I should have seen him but I wasn't paying attention. You need eyes in the back of your head.*

❻ What is the effect of the particular order of these sentences? (Think about the impact of the first short sentence, for example.)

ORGANISATION

In addition to considering the arrangement of smaller units like paragraphs, you will need to consider the structural integrity of the whole piece.

For example, are the events in a logical sequence? This could be a **chronological** or reverse chronological order. Many stories, told by a single narrator, proceed in the following **narrative arc**:

Stage in narrative arc	Explanation
Exposition: the start	a character is introduced in a particular situation
Rising action	we find out more about the situation – the main character faces obstacles and problems
Climax	the most dramatic or important moment – things could go either way.
Falling action	tension drops but things need to be explained or worked out
Resolution	the picture is clear or the truth is revealed – but this does not have to mean a 'happy ending'

❼ Think of any stories you know which follow this structure? (Fairy tales often fit this format.)

Many writers, however, experiment with the above structure. Ask yourself about the texts you study:

- Is there more than one narrator? Does the chronology change with each shift in voice? What is the effect of this?
- Are there **flashbacks**, which take the reader back to an event to shed light on what is happening in the present?
- Where does the narrative start and end? Sometimes they start in the middle (*in media res*) or at the end of the story.
- Is there a circular structure? Does the end reflect the beginning? If so, what is the effect of this?

APPLYING YOUR SKILLS   (A02)

The **novella** *A Christmas Carol* starts with Scrooge, now an old man, behaving in a mean way. He is then visited by several phantoms, the first taking him back in time. So, there are two time-lines:

- Scrooge, the old man, being shown the past, (and later the present and then the future)
- Events *in* the past, present and future

❽ Draw a time-line for any text you are studying (novels or plays). On one side, write the real time order of events. On the other note down, the order the events are *actually* presented in the text.

3.5 IMAGERY AND OTHER LITERARY TECHNIQUES

In both English Language and English Literature GCSEs, you will be given fiction and nonfiction extracts, poems and drama texts to comment on. In all cases, you will need to explore literary techniques and explain their effects using relevant terminology.

LITERARY DEVICES

Here are some of the most common literary devices:

Assonance – the repetition of vowel sounds, usually close together, to produce a particular effect, e.g. (from *Lotus-Eaters* by Alfred Tennyson): 'R<u>ou</u>nd and r<u>ou</u>nd the spicy d<u>ow</u>ns the yellow Lotus-dust is bl<u>ow</u>n.' The repetition of the 'o' suggests the swirling spirals of blown dust.

Alliteration – the repetition of a consonant usually, but not always, at the beginning of a word to emphasise, connect or contrast ideas, e.g. *Kubla Khan* by Samuel Taylor-Coleridge: 'Five <u>m</u>iles <u>m</u>eandering with a <u>m</u>azy <u>m</u>otion'. The alliteration of the repeated 'm' suggests the slow, convoluted passage of the river.

Personification – the giving of human qualities to non-living objects, e.g. (from *Anthem for Doomed Youth* by Wilfred Owen): 'Only the monstrous anger of the guns./Only the stuttering rifles' rapid rattle'. This humanises the horror of the killing, denoting it as a man-made catastrophe.

❶ Try reading out the second line by Wilfred Owen above. What does the alliteration of the 'r' sound suggest to you?

Onomatopoeia – the use of words describing sound, in which the actual sound of the words reflects what they are describing, for example, 'hiss' has a sibilant sound like a snake.

❷ Look again at the second line of the Wilfred Owen example and identify the two onomatopoeic words? What is the effect of using these?

TOP TIP

Onomatopoeia only applies to words that describe sounds. It usually makes writing more vivid by giving it an aural dimension.

IMAGERY

Imagery is a collective term referring to the use of language in a **figurative** or non-literal way, which creates pictures through words in the reader's mind. Similes and metaphors are both types of imagery.

Simile – the direct comparison of one thing with another usually using 'as' or 'like', e.g. from (*There came a Wind like a Bugle* by Emily Dickinson): 'There came a Wind like a Bugle -/ It quivered through the Grass'. The comparison of the wind with a bugle suggests its high-pitched sound which might herald something.

Metaphor – a more complex image where one thing is described as if it is something else without the 'as' or 'like' of a simile, e.g. 'The stall-holders squawked raucously, displaying their lengths of brilliant fabric flamboyantly, seducing the passing customers into landing briefly, at their table.' Here the stall-holders are likened to birds trying to attract a mate, suggesting both the gender of the stall-holders and customers and the bright, eye-catching nature of the fabric and the noise of the market.

EXAM FOCUS

Consider this extract from *Ode to Autumn* by John Keats where the use of imagery and other literary devices to convey a particular picture of autumn have been identified.

> Assonance gives a soft sound and contributes to the languid pace. It also suggests the circular nature of the seasons and the inevitability of change

> Who hath not seen thee oft amid thy store?
> Sometimes whoever seeks abroad may find
> Thee sitting careless on a granary floor,
> Thy hair soft-lifted by the winnowing wind;

> Personification makes Autumn a woman in a grain store – a gentle, feminised vision of plenty

> Image suggests a kind, harmonious relationship with nature

❸ Write a sentence analysing the effect of the words 'winnowing wind' in the last line ('winnowing' means 'act of wind blowing through something, often leaving what is pure or essential behind').

APPLYING YOUR SKILLS   (A02)(A02)

❹ Read the following extract. Then write a paragraph about how the writer describes the impact of the weather.
- Identify the literary devices
- Comment on their effect

> *The rain fell in steel stair rods, battering the leaves and delicate foliage, turning the dusty dry dirt of the track ahead into orange sludge that plastered itself over our jeep. Then, just as quickly as it started, it stopped and there was a moment's silence. The water dripped off the canvas roof, the drops plopping generously onto the windscreen, the gift of a beneficent Mother Nature.*

3.6 POETIC STYLE AND STRUCTURE

In the English Literature GCSE you will be required to comment on how ideas are presented in poetry and to make comparisons between poems.

In addition to the literary techniques explored in 3.5, there are particular stylistic and structural aspects relating to poetry that you will need to be familiar with, among them **rhyme** and **rhythm**.

RHYME

Rhyme is the repetition of the same sound within words, often at the end of a line.

Labelling lines alphabetically, using 'a' to label the first rhyming word and any subsequent words that rhyme with it, 'b' when a second and different rhyming sound is introduced, etc., helps to identify the **rhyme scheme**.

Look at the example below from *Dover Beach* by Matthew Arnold.

The sea is calm to-night.	a
The tide is full, the moon lies fair	b
Upon the straits; on the French coast the light	a
Gleams and is gone; the cliffs of England stand	c
Glimmering and vast, out in the tranquil bay.	d
Come to the window, sweet is the night-air!	b
Only, from the long line of spray	d
Where the sea meets the moon-blanched land	c

In this case, analysing the rhyme scheme like this shows that the poem's complex rhyming does not interrupt the gentle flow of the words reminiscent of the ebbing and flowing waves.

Near rhyme is where the repeated sound is similar but not the same. Consider this example from Emily Brontë's *To Imagination*.

But thou art ever there to bring
The hovering visions back and breathe
New glories o'er the blighted spring
And call a lovelier life from death

There is a near rhyme in the repeated 'eath' – the first being the long 'EEEE' sound in 'breathe', and the second a shorter 'e' sound suggesting the finality of 'death'.

❶ How does the near rhyme compare with the effect of the full rhyme between 'bring' and 'spring'?

Internal rhyme is where the word that carries the rhyme occurs in the middle of the line and then also in the middle or at the end of a subsequent line. Consider this example from Shakespeare's *Macbeth* in which the witches are making a potion:

> *Double, double, toil and trouble,*
>
> *Fire burn, and cauldron bubble 4.1.20-21*

This use of internal rhyme suggests the swirling contents of the caldron as well as the deepening gravity of the difficulties brought on by Macbeth's actions. It is supported by the repeated sounds of double, trouble and bubble, which give the effect of an incantation.

❷ What internal rhymes can you identify in the following lines of poetry? Why do you think the poet chose this particular repeating sound?

> *The hyena's high-pitched cry*
> *Echoes round the city walls as*
> *Night lies down swift and dark.*
> *So daylight flies away in fear.*
>
> Mike Gould

TOP TIP

If there is a regular rhyming pattern and this is broken or changed, make sure you examine it closely to find out why and explain the effect it creates.

RHYTHM

In poetry a crafted pattern of stressed and unstressed **syllables** and words, gives the lines a beat or rhythm. The use of rhyme also contributes to this. One example of poetic rhythm, which is found in many poems and in Shakespearian verse, comes through the use of **Iambic pentameter**. Here syllables alternate between unstressed and stressed beats. Each unstressed/stressed unit or foot is called an **iamb** and 'pentameter' means there are five feet in a line.

AIMING HIGH

Maximise use of quotations to explain multiple features and their effects. For example, in the quotation from *Macbeth* you would comment on what the alliteration and the assonance add to the impact of the lines.

Consider this example from *Romeo and Juliet*:

Two households both alike in dignity
In fair Verona where we lay our scene

1. Prologue. 1–2

Now look at how these lines can be marked in terms of unstressed and stressed beats:

˘ Two	ˊ house	˘ holds	ˊ both	˘ a	ˊ like	˘ in	ˊ dig	˘ nit	ˊ y
˘ In	ˊ fair	˘ Ver	ˊ on	˘ a	ˊ where	˘ we	ˊ lay	˘ our	ˊ scene

In the first line, the rhythm helps to create meaning, with the stressed syllables (/) emphasising the similar high-standing of both families and so implying that what happens between them will have a significant impact.

❸ What is emphasised by the stressed syllables in the second line? What message does it help convey to the audience about setting?

❹   Consider the following two lines from *Macbeth,* when Macbeth meets his deadliest enemy. Which words are empathised by the rhythm and what is the effect of this?

> *Of all men else I have avoided thee,*
> *But get thee back, my soul is too much charged*

Blank verse is unrhymed iambic pentameter and is given to the ordinary characters in Shakespeare's plays, whilst those of rank often speak in rhyming iambic pentameter to indicate their higher status.

Free verse is a very open form of poetry without a regular rhyme pattern or rhythm, but which evokes natural speech. For example in these lines from 'The Simple Truth' by Philip Levine:

> *Some things*
> *you know all your life. They are so simple and true*
> *they must be said without elegance, meter and rhyme,*
> *they must be laid on the table beside the salt shaker*

Here simplicity of form reflects the simple truths of the poem and so communicates its message directly.

FORM

Form refers to a poem's particular shape and structure.

Stanzas– poetry is often divided into these separate sections to indicate:

- A change of subject or a shift in meaning within the same general subject
- A progression within the subject or narrative (e.g. time)
- A change of tone or mood
- A pause/a moment for reflection

Punctuation and capitalisation – some poems start each line with a capital letter and end with punctuation and others have neither. Some lines flow into the next line, referred to as **enjambment**, while others stop at the end. Again, you need to consider the effect of these features.

❺   Look again at the short poem extract on page 47 about the hyenas.

   a) Where has enjambment been used?

   b) Which line(s) are complete sentences?

There are some particular forms or types of poetry that demand a specific structure and rhyme pattern, for example a **sonnet**. This is a poem of fourteen lines, in iambic pentameter, often ending (as with the **Shakespearian sonnet**) in a **rhyming couplet**. It is traditionally a poem of thwarted love and courtship.

TOP TIP

Always look at the shape of a poem on the page and comment. Are any stanzas (or verses) longer than others? Are the lines of differing lengths?

However, all poems have a form – a shape. Read the following short **elegy** by Mary Coleridge.

> On such a day
> Some hang above the tombs,
> Some weep in empty rooms,
> I, when the iris blooms,
> 5   Remember.
>
> I, when the cyclamen
> Opens her buds again,
> Rejoice a moment – then
>   Remember

❻ This poem is about mourning and remembering someone who has died.

Why do you think Mary Coleridge has:

- Made the poem in this shape
- Split the poem in two (the second stanza focuses on something different)
- Chosen these short, concise little verses
- Used a **refrain**, by repeating the word 'Remember' separately? (How does it affect the reader?)

APPLYING YOUR SKILLS   **A02**

❼ Consider the following extract from *Meeting at Night* by Elizabeth Barrett Browning.

How does the writer build excitement in the following lines, through:

- the subject and tone
- rhyme scheme and structure
- personification
- alliteration?

> The grey sea and the long black land;
> And the yellow half-moon large and low;
> And the startled little waves that leap
> In fiery ringlets from their sleep,
> 5   As I gain the cove with pushing prow,
> And quench its speed i' the slushy sand.
>
> Then a mile of warm sea-scented beach;
> Three fields to cross till a farm appears;
> A tap at the pane, the quick sharp scratch
> 10 And blue spurt of a lighted match,
> And a voice less loud, thro' its joys and fears,
> Than the two hearts beating each to each!

3.7 DRAMATIC STYLE AND STRUCTURE

For English Literature GCSE you will need to be able to analyse playwrights' choices and how dramatic techniques have been used for particular effect.

ACTS AND SCENES

Plays are divided into acts, which are usually defined by the key plot developments, and sub-divided into scenes. The location of these breaks in action contributes to the building of meaning in a drama.

In Shakespeare's *Macbeth* for example, the first scenes of Act One move between different worlds, shedding light but also contrasting with each other. The ethereal witches' scene is followed by the realities of warfare in the second scene. They are linked by the predictions of the witches.

Entrances and exits – the way that characters enter and exit the stage can tell us further information about them and their role in the play. The beginning of Shakespeare's *Macbeth*, starts with:

> *Thunder and lightning. Enter three WITCHES*

The fact that the witches are the first characters to appear immediately suggests their importance in the play, and their entrance with thunder and lightning implies their sinister impact on future events.

Similarly, in J. B. Priestley's, *An Inspector Calls,* entrances and exits play a significant role in deepening meaning. For example, this **stage direction** from Act One, when the Inspector shows Sheila a photograph of the dead girl whom he is investigating.

> *She looks at it closely, recognises it with a little cry, gives a half-stifled sob, and then runs out.*

❶ What might the key actions, highlighted here, suggest about how Sheila feels?

TOP TIP

When considering stage directions and setting, be sure to identify what extra information may be conveyed by them.

STAGING

Where plays are set, provides another way for the playwright to develop characters and themes. Consider the effect of each setting outlined below:

Play/focus	Setting	Effect of setting
Romeo and Juliet – Conflict and love between the Capulet and Montague families	Act 1 Scene 1: *Verona a public place*	Implies the wider/public impact of the conflict between the two families
An Inspector Calls – Social status versus social conscience	Act 1: Birlings' house – *substantial and heavily comfortable but not cosy and homelike*	Suggests the brash, unwelcoming nature of the family and the absence of values underneath the face they show to the wider world.

SPEECH AND MOVEMENT DIRECTIONS

These indications of how certain lines should be delivered, usually provided in brackets, often offer more information about a character. Read this example from *An Inspector Calls*, where Birling is talking about women to his future son-in-law, Gerald, with his son, Eric, listening.

> BIRLING: Yes, but you've got to remember, my boy, that clothes mean something different to a woman. Not just something to wear – and not only something to make 'em look prettier – but – well, a sort of sign or token of their self-respect.
>
> GERALD: That's true.
>
> ERIC [*eagerly*]: Yes, I remember – [*but he checks himself*]
>
> BIRLING: Well, what do you remember?
>
> ERIC [*confused*]: Nothing.

❷ What do the highlighted speech directions indicate about Eric?

Similarly, movement or gesture directions to the actors about what to do on stage are often revealing about characters. Consider the following:

> BIRLING: I see. Sensible really. [*Moves restlessly, then turns.*] You've had enough of that Port Eric.
>
> [*The* INSPECTOR *is watching* BIRLING *and now* BIRLING *notices him.*]
>
> INSPECTOR: I think you remember Eva Smith now, don't you, Mr Birling?

Birling's movements suggests his uneasy conscience and the Inspector's close observation of him reveals that the Inspector knows more than he's saying.

APPLYING YOUR SKILLS   (A02)

Read the following extract from *An Inspector Calls*. Sheila's involvement in the circumstances leading up to the suicide of a young woman have just been revealed and Gerald's involvement is about to be exposed by the Inspector.

> *ACT TWO*
>
> *At rise, scene and situation are exactly as they were at end of Act One.*
>
> [*The INSPECTOR remains at the door for a few moments looking at SHEILA and GERALD. Then he comes forward, leaving door open behind him.*]
>
> INSPECTOR: Well?
>
> SHEILA [*with hysterical laugh, to* GERALD]: You see? What did I tell you?
>
> INSPECTOR [*to* GERALD]: What did you tell him?
>
> GERALD [*with an effort*]: Inspector, I think Miss Birling ought to be excused any more of this questioning.

❸ Write a paragraph explaining what the stage, speech and movement directions tell us about:

   a) Sheila and Gerald's state of mind

   b) The Inspector's control of the situation

3.8 EVALUATING TEXTS

It is important for English Language GCSE that you are able to evaluate texts critically.

WHAT IS EVALUATION?

Evaluating texts means determining a text's success or effectiveness in terms of what the writer set out to achieve. In the exam this might involve analysing the presentation of a character, an issue or how a tension or a particular mood is created in a text.

You might be asked the extent to which you agree with a particular opinion about a text. Consider the following extract from *Great Expectations* by Charles Dickens. Pip, the narrator, as a young boy is living with his older sister and her husband Joe.

A typical question might be: 'A student reading this passage has written: "Dickens has created a convincing picture of Joe's childlike nature." To what extent do you agree?'

> *'Well,' said Joe, glancing up at the Dutch clock, 'she's been on the Ram-page, this last spell, about five minutes, Pip. She's a coming! Get behind the door, old chap, and have the jack-towel betwixt you.'*
>
> *I took the advice. My sister, Mrs. Joe, throwing the door wide open, and finding an obstruction behind it, immediately divined the cause, and applied Tickler to its further investigation. She concluded by throwing me – I often served her as a connubial missile – at Joe, who, glad to get hold of me on any terms, passed me on into the chimney and quietly fenced me up there with his great leg.*

Planning points for this evaluation might look like this:

Agree:

- Joe's use of language such as 'Ram-page' and 'She's a coming' are child-like in their simplicity.
- Joe addresses Pip as 'old chap' as if he were an equal.
- Joe seems unable to prevent the violence of Mrs Joe towards Pip.

Disagree:

- Joe rapidly evaluates the situation and suggests a quick, practical solution, 'have the jack-towel betwixt you.'
- Joe uses his adult frame to shield Pip, 'fenced me up there with his great leg.'

❶ Complete this student's evaluation.

I feel that the picture of Joe as childlike is convincing/unconvincing because...

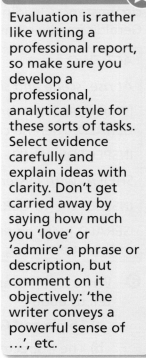

AIMING HIGH ⭐

Evaluation is rather like writing a professional report, so make sure you develop a professional, analytical style for these sorts of tasks. Select evidence carefully and explain ideas with clarity. Don't get carried away by saying how much you 'love' or 'admire' a phrase or description, but comment on it objectively: 'the writer conveys a powerful sense of ...', etc.

Read this extract from *The Diary of a Nobody* by George and Weedon Grossmith, first published in the late 1800s. It depicts English Victorian suburban life from the point of view of Charles Pooter, a city clerk. Charles is attending a Mansion House dinner, with his wife Carrie, at the invitation of the Lord and Lady Mayoress.

> *Carrie made a most hearty supper, for which I was pleased; for I sometimes think she is not strong. There was scarcely a dish she did not taste. I was so thirsty, I could not eat much. Receiving a sharp slap on the shoulder, I turned, and, to my amazement, saw Farmerson our ironmongers. He said, in the most familiar way: 'This is better than Brickfield Terrace, eh?' I simply looked at him, and said coolly; 'I never expected to see you here.'*

② How well does the writer convey social and gender relationships? Consider:

    a) the view of women as presented in the opening sentence

    b) Charles's attitude to seeing the ironmongers at the dinner.

APPLYING YOUR SKILLS

③ Read the following extract from a gothic mystery story. Evaluate how well a feeling of tension and menace have been generated.

> *The bell jangled, echoing oddly, like someone laughing hysterically, and the heavy door slowly opened onto a gloomy hallway that smelt of damp. A wary, white face raised a quizzical eyebrow. I found myself stammering.*
>   *'I'm, I'm looking for a Tom Masters. I understand he rents the basement flat.'*
>   *'He left some time ago', the voice was strangely quiet, 'and there's no forwarding address.'*

PROGRESS CHECK FOR CHAPTER THREE

GOOD PROGRESS

I can:

- Compare writers' ideas and perspectives, across different texts and contexts ☐
- Evaluate texts critically and support this with appropriate textual references ☐
- Explain, using appropriate terminology, how language, form and structure create meaning and effects ☐

EXCELLENT PROGRESS

I can:

- Compare writers' ideas and perspectives thoughtfully and in detail across different texts engaging with appropriate contexts ☐
- Evaluate texts critically and exploratively with a range of well-selected references ☐
- Analyse language, form and structure showing insight into the way they create meaning and effects ☐

4.1 WHAT IS COMPARISON?

In both English Language and English Literature GCSEs you will be required to compare texts. In English Language this will be between non-fiction and literary non-fiction texts, and in English Literature it will be a comparison between poems.

COMPARING SIMILARITIES AND DIFFERENCES

A textual comparison involves the careful consideration of the similarities and differences between one text and another. In most cases, you will be asked to focus on a particular issue, idea or experience. For example, 'How do the two writers convey their different experiences of growing up or leaving home?'

The features that you comment on will vary according to the type of text but, you will usually need to:

- **Compare** the different perspectives (what each writer thinks or feels about the issue or experience)
- **Support** your ideas with well-chosen evidence or examples from the text/s
- **Analyse** the language and structure carefully and how the writers get their views across

TOP TIP

Focus on the most obvious similarities/ differences first, and then move on to the more subtle examples as you will have limited time and two texts to read.

❶ Read these two short extracts about perspectives on Christmas. How do the writers' views and approaches compare?

Writer A	Writer B
... draw your chair nearer the blazing fire – fill the glass and send round the song...	Tensions, buried beneath the mound of school routine, work and geographical distance, can be forced to the surface.

EXAM FOCUS

Now read what one student has written:

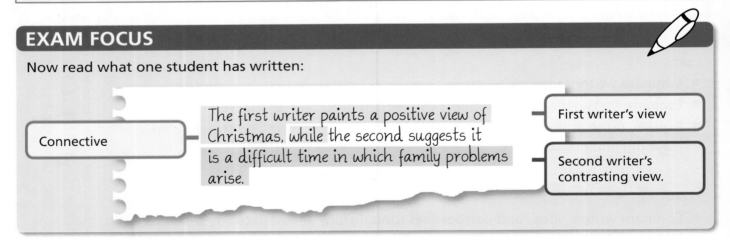

Connective

The first writer paints a positive view of Christmas, while the second suggests it is a difficult time in which family problems arise.

First writer's view

Second writer's contrasting view.

❷ Select the best words or phrases (not the whole text) from each example to support the points the student makes.

❸ Now, analyse the language choices. For example, you could comment on:

- the imagery of the first example (what effect phrases such as 'blazing fire' and 'fill the glass' create)

or

- the impact of the metaphor of the problems 'buried beneath the mound of...'.

Now read the remainder of each extract below. Extract A is from *A Christmas Dinner – Sketches by Boz* by Charles Dickens and Extract B is an extract from a newspaper article.

Extract A	Extract B
... draw your chair nearer the blazing fire – fill the glass and send round the song – and, if your room be smaller than it was a dozen years ago, or if your glass be filled with reeking punch, instead of sparkling wine, put a good face on the matter, and empty it off-hand, and fill another, and troll off the old ditty you used to sing, and thank God it's no worse. Look on the merry faces of your children as they sit round the fire. One little seat may be empty – one slight form that gladdened the father's heart, and roused the mother's pride to look upon, may not be there. Dwell not upon the past	If you look at the Christmas adverts on TV and the glossy pictures adorning magazine covers, you'd be forgiven for thinking that every family celebrates Christmas in a haze of happiness and silly Christmas jumpers. The truth is often quite different. Tensions, buried beneath the mound of school routine, work and geographical distance, can be forced to the surface. Financial constraints, sibling rivalries and over-indulgence can all strain the feelings of peace and goodwill. There is a reason that lawyers nickname the first working Monday after the Christmas break, 'Divorce Day'.

APPLYING YOUR SKILLS

❹ Make notes on:

- Any further points or perspectives each writer has on Christmas in each extract
- Any suitable quotations to support the points you want to make
- The effect of any of these words or phrases (if you can, comment on their specific use)

4.2 ANALYSING LANGUAGE FOR COMPARISON

Unit 4.1 introduced some basic techniques that writers use to convey differing viewpoints, but for higher levels you will need to analyse their language choices closely, but concisely.

You could use the following memory-aid (**WISPS**) to help you with your comparison:

- **W**ords and phrases – how vocabulary is used for particular effect
- **I**magery – the use of imagery and other literary devices
- **S**entence structure and length
- **P**aragraphing and organisation
- **S**tyle and tone of the extracts

For example, read this extract from *Factory Children* by Cavie Richardson relating to new laws to limit working hours for factory children in the 1800s.

❶ **a)** What is the viewpoint on child labour? What evidence is there to support your answer?

> *The Factory System [...] reduces the Child of the poor Citizen to the rank of an animal machine – to the condition of a breathing automaton. Suns shine, and flowers bloom, and forests wave, and streams run glittering in the light, in vain for the tens and thousands of British Children condemned to the incessant labours of the Factory. The glorious God of Nature is almost put out of the imaginations of these poor martyrs and avarice, and man's puny arts alone fill their minds, gas and steam are the only elements of power and light with which they are acquainted – potatoes and oatmeal the only viands with which they are familiar – broken rest, severe punishment, excessive toil, the only usage to which they are accustomed.*

One student has identified this point of view in the text:

- Child labour dehumanises children

b) Find evidence to support this view. Can you identify at least one more point made relating to this view and locate evidence in the text.

CONVEYING VIEWPOINT THROUGH LANGUAGE

To make a detailed analysis, you need to really *zoom in* on the use of language for example, by identifying the words and phrases that tell us about things in life the factory child is missing out on.

❷ Add two more words or phrases to this list taken from the extract:
- 'Suns shine'
- 'Flowers bloom'

ANALYSE FOR SUCCESS

Next you need to analyse the word choice carefully. For example, here are some **connotations** which come to mind from the chosen vocabulary:

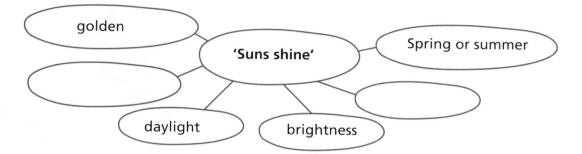

❸ Add one or two more words or ideas that come into your mind from the phrase 'Suns shine'.

❹ Now create your own diagram (or word list, if you prefer) for one of the other words or phrases you selected. (You won't have time in the exam to do this, but it is useful to think in this way.)

THE IMPACT OF IMAGERY

Some of the words or phrases you chose will have shown the writer's use of imagery but there are some even stronger ones in the text. For example, the writer says that children who work in factories can be compared to:

- An 'animal machine'
- A 'breathing automaton'

❺ Which of the following interpretations is closest to what the author meant here?

   a) The factory is like a panting animal.

   b) There is too much technology and equipment in factories.

   c) Children become dehumanised and behave like robots.

EXAM FOCUS

Here is one student's attempt to write about the use of vocabulary and imagery in the passage:

> The writer feels that the factory system has a terrible impact on children's humanity, making them 'animal machines'. The metaphor suggests that they become part of the whole factory as if swallowed up by it. Because of this they will miss out on the pleasures of nature and fresh air, where . . .

❻ Copy and complete the paragraph, adding relevant evidence and analysis based on the work you have just done.

SENTENCES AND STRUCTURE

The variety of sentences and the use of paragraphs are also very important in understanding viewpoint and being able to compare texts. For example:

> The Factory System [...] *reduces the Child of the poor Citizen to the rank of an animal machine – to the condition of a breathing automaton.*

This is a **topic sentence**. It introduces the key viewpoint explaining that children are dehumanised or 'reduced.'

The sentences that follow **add detail** and use **rhetorical devices** to create impact. For example:

> *'Suns shine, and flowers bloom, and forests wave, and streams run glittering in the light, in vain for the tens and thousands of British Children condemned to the incessant labours of the Factory.*

Here the repetition of 'and' builds up a wave of images which it is difficult to ignore.

The final long sentence introduces new ideas and uses similar structural devices to make an impact:

| Links back to images of fresh air and sunshine | *The glorious God of Nature is almost put out of the imaginations of these poor martyrs and avarice, and man's puny arts alone fill their minds, gas and steam are the only elements of power and light with which they are acquainted - potatoes and oatmeal the only viands with which they are familiar - broken rest, severe punishment, excessive toil, the only usage to which they are accustomed.* | Introduces the realities of factory life |
| Pattern of three stresses the awful conditions | | |

❼ What repeated two words (they appear three times) emphasise the children's hardships?

STYLE AND TONE

It is also important to try to sum up or convey the overall mood or tone of the passage, based on its style. For example, one student has written:

> The writer uses a hard-hitting, emotive tone that engages the reader's sympathies for children's sufferings and creates a powerful contrast between factory life and the natural world.

❽ How accurate a summary of the tone of the extract do you think this is?

❾ Now read this short text on a similar topic.

> *To see the bright, shiny line of new cars assembled by a dazzling line of human-like robots, is to see the future. No mess, no danger, no people.*

Write your own short summary of the tone of this text.

> **TOP TIP** ⭐
>
> Not all of the **WISPS** features will be significant in every extract, so comment on the most obvious devices that contribute to conveying the viewpoint for that particular text.

PUTTING IT ALL TOGETHER

Now read the following, describing two events – the first, the Great Fire of London in 1666 and the second, the annual bonfire and parades in the Sussex town of Lewes. Read both texts, thinking about their different perspectives on fire.

Extract A

Oh the miserable and calamitous spectacle, such as haply the world had not seen since the foundation of it, nor be outdone till the universal conflagration thereof. All the sky was of a fiery aspect, like the top of a burning oven, and the light seen above 40 miles round about for many nights. God grant mine eyes may never behold the like, who now saw above 10,000 houses all in one flame; the noise and cracking and thunder of people, the fall of towers, houses, and churches, was like an hideous storm, and the air all about so hot and inflamed that at last one was not able to approach it, so that they were forced to stand still and let the flames burn on, which they did for near two miles in length and one in breadth. The clouds also of smoke were dismal and reached upon computation near 50 miles in length. Thus I left it this afternoon burning, a resemblance of Sodom, or the last day. It forcibly called to my mind that passage—non enim hic habemus stabilem civitatum: the ruins resembling the picture of Troy. London was, but is no more!

John Evelyn

Extract B

Although the Lewes bonfire, like all bonfires, commemorates the Gunpowder Plot, this is not really about the bonfires themselves (yes, there are several in the town each year). No, this is about celebration, not destruction. For months before the big day, bonfire 'societies' based on local villages or parts of the town raise money for their costumes so that when the time comes, they can march proudly through the streets, warmed by the flaming crosses and poles they hold, or swept along by the lively music played by the marching bands. The fires onto which they ceremoniously throw their torches at the end of the parade are a visible reminder of local community, local pride and local unity.

Mike Gould

⑩   Make notes on:
- the different viewpoints expressed in each extract
- suitable quotations to evidence these points and your analysis.

APPLYING YOUR SKILLS   (A03)

⑪   Write at least two paragraphs (one on each extract) comparing how the writers have conveyed their different views and experiences of fires.

   Use the WISPS points to comment on the language and structure use in each text.

4.3 COMPARING POEMS

For English Literature GCSE you need to be able to compare and contrast poems making relevant connections between them.

HOW TO APPROACH MAKING A COMPARISON

First, read these two poems which both relate to the poet's view of Nature. As you do so, apply the same skills as you might for analysing prose extracts – looking for evidence of the writers' perspectives and the language used to convey these.

TOP TIP

Similarly to other comparison questions, the poems are likely to be on a related theme or topic but will approach the subject in different ways.

Poem A: 'Nature's Questioning' by Thomas Hardy

> When I look forth at dawning, pool,
> Field, flock, and lonely tree,
> All seem to gaze at me
> 4   Like chastened children sitting silent in a school;
>
> Their faces dulled, constrained, and worn,
> As though the master's ways
> Through the long teaching days
> 8   Had cowed them till their early zest was over-borne.
>
> Upon them stirs in lippings¹ mere
> (As if once clear in call,
> But now scarce breathed at all) –
> 12   'We wonder, ever wonder, why we find us here!
>
> 'Has some vast imbecility,
> Mighty to build and blend,
> But impotent to tend,
> 16   Framed us in jest, and left us now to hazardry?
>
> 'Or come we of an automaton
> Unconscious of our pains?
> Or are we live remains
> 20   Of Godhead dying downwards, brain and eye now gone?
> 'Or is it that some high plan betides
> As yet not understood,
> Of evil stormed by good,
> 24   We the forlorn hope over which achievements strides?'
>
> Thus things around, No answerer I...
> Meanwhile the winds, and rains,
> And earth's old glooms and pains
> 28   Are still the same, and life and death are neighbours nigh.

Glossary:
¹ *lippings* – whisperings

Poem B: 'Pied Beauty' by Gerard Manley Hopkins

> Glory be to God for dappled things –
> For skies of couple-colour as a brinded cow;
> For rose-moles all in stipple upon trout that swim;
> Fresh-firecoal chestnut-falls[1]; finches' wings;
> 5   Landscape plotted[2] and pieced – fold, fallow and plough;
> And all trades, their gear and tackle trim.
>
> All things counter[3], original, spare, strange;
> Whatever is fickle, freckled (who knows how?)
> With swift, slow; sweet, sour; adazzle, dim;
> 10   He fathers-forth[4] whose beauty is past change: Praise him.

Glossary:
[1] *Fresh-firecoal chestnuts fall* – when chestnuts fall from the tree, bursting their husks they are as bright as burning coal
[2] *plotted* – divided
[3] *counter* – contrary
[4] *fathers-forth* – moves creatively onwards

Now read this exam-style task:

> **Both poets write about Nature and the feelings it evokes in them. What are the similarities and differences in the ways the poets present these feelings?**

STAGE 1: STARTING – THE OVERALL VIEWPOINT

❶ Read both poems and on a separate piece of paper, jot down what you think is the *general* view of Nature in each case? At this point, this can be an overall impression which you will look to support with evidence from annotations.

For example, which of the two poets' attitudes seems troubled and sad? Which seems joyful and wondrous? Can you find any evidence for these attitudes?

STAGE 2: ANNOTATING THE POEMS

In the exam, you may have already annotated or made notes on the first poem, but if not you will need to do that for both poems. You should consider annotating:

● Any particular words or phrases that stand out or create impact

● Any specific language devices you recognise (imagery, alliteration etc.)

● Any structural features – how the poem/s are split up in terms of stanzas or other patterns or shapes you notice, such as repeated ideas or rhyming words or lines

❷ Make these notes or annotations, keeping in mind your general impression of the poets' views (but be prepared to change if the evidence points in another direction).

EXAM FOCUS

One student has made these initial annotations/notes on vocabulary and sound effects:

- Word choices across the two poems:

  'Field, flock, and lonely tree,' presents a slightly forlorn picture in Poem A?

  Poem B – 'fold, fallow and plough', more harmonious?

- Use of imagery:

  Natural features of the countryside – 'Like chastened children sitting silent in a school;' simile sounds like punishment by God?

  'For skies of couple-colour as a brinded cow', more harmonious simile, down to earth view of nature in Poem B?

- Alliteration and/or assonance:

  Repetition of the 'w' in, 'We wonder, ever wonder, why we find us here!', reinforces the tone of questioning in Poem A; but in Poem B, repetition of the 'g' in, 'Glory be to God for dappled things' is celebratory, like a hymn.

❸ Write up one of these points in a paragraph of your own. You could start:

In Poem A, the poet seems to present a...

STRUCTURE

You also need to comment on how structure supports or develops the differences in meaning. For example, here are some further notes made by the same student:

- Similarities or differences in the use of punctuation:

  The use of long sentences in poem A creates a thoughtful tone but an aside in parentheses, '(As if once clear in call, / But now scarce breathed at all) – 'and dashes create a sense of questioning uncertainty which contrasts with poem B. Here an aside is used to suggest lack of certainty is a good thing '(who knows how?)' and dashes couple words together 'Fresh- recoal chestnut-fall' strengthening their impact.

TOP TIP

You may not have time under exam conditions to analyse all the poetic devices, so choose those that best support your comparison and then expand your comments to other features.

- Similarities/differences in layout on the page or form:

  Poem A uses a conventional layout of seven stanza of equal length which contrasts with the unconventional approach of questioning religious certainty whereas Poem B has a rather more unconventional shortness with two stanzas of unequal length for a more conventional purpose: praising God.

- Compare the use of rhythm and rhyme:

  Poem A has a regular rhythm and rhyme facilitating its thoughtfulness, whereas Poem B uses the same rhyming sounds between stanzas to closely connect the sentiments, uniting it as a hymn of praise.

APPLYING YOUR SKILLS   (A01) (A02)

④ Now, reread the main task:

> **Both poets write about Nature and the feelings it evokes in them. What are the similarities and differences in the ways the poets present these feelings?**

Taking **only** the final stanza of each of the two poems, compare the ways the poets present their feelings about nature here.

Remember:

- Comment on the viewpoints.
- Support your points with evidence.
- Analyse and comment on the uses of language and structure (in each case).

PROGRESS CHECK FOR CHAPTER FOUR

GOOD PROGRESS

I can:

- Identify and compare viewpoints in non-fiction texts and how language has been used to convey them ☐
- Compare two poems considering their subject and tone together with how language and structure have been used to convey meaning ☐

EXCELLENT PROGRESS

I can:

- Make insightful comparison of viewpoints in non-fiction texts and analyse the range of ways language has been used to convey them ☐
- Show a detailed, sophisticated understanding of the relationship between poems, comparing the use of linguistic and structural devices to convey meaning ☐

5.1 DECODING THE QUESTION

Once you have mastered the reading skills required for English and English Literature GCSEs, the next stage is to put them into practice under exam conditions.

Follow these steps:

- Be prepared. Ensure that you know the format of each exam paper; how many questions you need to answer and what type they are likely to be.
- Read the instructions on the front of the paper to remind yourself of what you need to do. This is something you can do while you are waiting for the exam to begin.
- Manage the time you have well by being clear about the number of questions, their value in marks and work out how much time you can spend on each question, then sticking to this.

THE PROCESS INVOLVED AND CONTENT OF THE QUESTION

First, make sure you understand exactly what you are being asked to do. Questions consist of two main parts: the content and the process involved.

> **The content** – this is the '**what** you have been asked to write about'. Make sure you focus specifically on the topic in the task.
>
> Only cover the part of the text that is specified. If this is a section of an extract, mark it off on the question paper. If one extract is part of a longer piece and the other extract is a whole piece, note this, as it could affect your comments on structural aspects.

> **The process involved** – parts of the question will indicate exactly what you have **to do**. Some common process terms are as follows (most are action words but some are questions words):
>
> - Analyse – examine in detail to establish meanings and key features
> - Describe – provide a detailed account or picture of something
> - Explain – give a reasoned account that clarifies something
> - Evaluate – form a judgement about the effectiveness of something
> - Identify – find key points or features
> - Summarise – a brief account of the main issues or points
> - Consider – look attentively and think carefully about something
> - Compare – examine the similarities or differences between things
> - Contrast – explore differences between two texts and ideas
> - List – Make a series of brief points

TOP TIP

If you've been provided with guidance (usually in bullet point form) as to what your response should include, it's important to use this to structure your answer.

Read the question below, paying careful attention to the completed annotations:

Q1 – Focus this part of your answer on the second part of the Source from **line 19 to the end**. [1]

A critic, having read this section of the text said: 'The writer's characters are exaggerated and unreal.' [2]

To what extent do you agree? [3]

In your response, you could:

- Write about [4] your own impressions of the characters [5]
- Identify how [6] the writer has created these impressions [7] and evaluate [8] the effect on the characters overall [9]
- Support your opinions with references to the text. [10]

[20 marks]

---

[1] Content   [2] Content   [3] Process

[4] Process   [5] Content   [6] Process

❶ Now decide for yourself whether each of the four remaining highlighted parts of the question are 'content' or 'process'.

JUDGING YOUR RESPONSE AGAINST THE NUMBER OF MARKS

Answer length – The number of marks awarded and the time allowed will give you a clear guide as to how long the answers need to be.

For example, if you have been asked to list four things and there are four marks, you only need to write sufficient to justify a mark for each. If a question has thirty marks then a substantial response will be required.

Planning and checking – It is always best to:

- Make a brief plan before start writing as it will focus your response and improve the structure. Spend no more than 5 minutes on this for a longer response and 2 minutes for a shorter one
- Check that the planned response directly addresses the question and tick off the points on the plan as you write them
- Neatly cross out the plan to show that it is not part of the answer

Also allow a few minutes at the end to check back through your answers for spelling or grammar errors. Remember that 20% of your marks for English Language and 5% of the marks for English Literature are awarded for spelling punctuation and grammar.

APPLYING YOUR SKILLS

❷ Consider the question below and identify the content and process words:

Starting with the above speech, explain how Shakespeare presents attitudes towards women in this play.

Write about:

- what is said about women in this speech
- how Shakespeare presents attitudes towards women in the play as a whole.

5.2 READING UNSEEN PASSAGES

All of your texts in the English Language GCSE will be ones that you are unlikely to have seen or studied before. It is therefore important that you are fully prepared to approach these 'unseen' texts.

APPROACHING FICTION AND NON-FICTION EXTRACTS

When you are presented with an unseen extract in the exam, first read the question carefully in the manner suggested in the previous unit, identifying the content and process words. Also look at the marks awarded to the question and consider carefully how much time you can allow to answer it.

First reading: ideally in the exam, you should read the unseen texts at least twice. The first reading should be a quick reading that establishes the following:

- The overall subject – this is *what* it is about
- The meaning – this is *how* the subject has been treated
- The tone – this is the *manner* in which it has been explored
- Any outstanding features in relation to the question asked – is there anything that you immediately notice when you read the piece?

If the question is a very brief one, with a few marks, for example, where you are asked to list four things about a particular feature, skim through the text identifying what specifically you need to answer the question.

Second reading: if the question is a more detailed one, the second reading should be a careful one that targets the details that you'll need to analyse in order to respond to the question you've been asked. Annotate the text as you go. Depending on the type of text and what you've been asked to do, you may need to consider the following in addition to the information gleaned at the first reading:

- Viewpoint
- Particular vocabulary
- Sentence and paragraph length and structure
- Linguistic devices
- Form and structure of the piece
- Explicit and implicit information

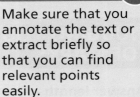

TOP TIP

Make sure that you annotate the text or extract briefly so that you can find relevant points easily.

TOP TIP

Everyone reads at different speeds and if you are a slow reader, you may want to read the text just once, very carefully, annotating as you go.

Consider the following question and extract from *The Hound of the Baskervilles* by Sir Arthur Conan Doyle which appears near the start of the book, when Dr Watson and the heir of Baskerville Hall, a lonely ancestral house on the moors, arrive for the first time.

List **four** things from this extract about the environment surrounding the house, on the moor

[4 marks]

I drew aside my curtains before I went to bed and looked out from my window. It opened upon the grassy space which lay in front of the hall door. Beyond, two copses of trees moaned [1] and swung in a rising wind. [6] A half moon broke through the rifts of racing [3] clouds. [2] In its cold [2] light I saw beyond the trees a broken fringe of rocks, and the long, low curve of the melancholy [4] moor. [3] I closed the curtain, feeling that my last impression was in keeping with the rest.

*   And yet it was not quite the last. [5] I found myself weary and yet wakeful, tossing restlessly from side to side, seeking for the sleep [3] which would not come. Far away a chiming clock struck [6] out the quarters of the hours, but otherwise a deathly [4] silence lay upon the old house. [5] And then, suddenly, in the very dead [4] of the night, there came a sound to my ears, clear, resonant [6] and unmistakeable. It was the sob [1] of a woman, the muffled, strangling gasp [1] of one who is torn by an uncontrollable sorrow. [4]*

A student has started to highlight the extract in yellow and green and has noted two of the four aspects below:

- There is grass in front of the house
- There are two copses of trees

❶ Identify two more examples of aspects of the environment around the house.

A further question about the same extract asks the following:

Look in detail at the extract.

How does the writer use language here to set a sinister tone?

You could include the writer's choice of:
- words and phrases
- language features and techniques
- sentence forms.

[8 marks]

The same student has underlined and numbered some features in the extract and has identified the first two.

1 onomatopoeia – use of language to amplify the sinister sounds
2 pathetic fallacy – weather that reflects the general mood
3
4

❷ Make notes to identify the features in annotations 3 to 6.

5.3 READING UNSEEN POEMS

In English Literature GCSE you will be asked to comment on poems you may not have seen before. It can be helpful to develop a systematic approach to this.

HOW TO APPROACH AN 'UNSEEN' POEM

To help fully understand poetry, imagine it being spoken as you read it. Ideally, you will need to read it at least twice. On the first reading, focus on the meaning using these prompts:

- What is the story or subject of the poem?
- What is the tone of the poem: sad, reflective, joyous or angry?
- Are there any particular features that stand out?

The second time, read it slowly and carefully, considering:

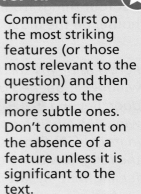

TOP TIP

Comment first on the most striking features (or those most relevant to the question) and then progress to the more subtle ones. Don't comment on the absence of a feature unless it is significant to the text.

Language used to create the meaning and tone	Structure used to develop of the meaning and tone
• Any particular words that stand out • Use of similes and metaphors • Onomatopoeic words • Use of alliteration and assonance • Personification • Voice	• Form • Punctuation • Enjambment • Rhythm and rhyme • Repetition • Stanzas and their order

FIRST READING

Read the poem, 'My Boy Jack' by Rudyard Kipling, below once. Imagine you have been asked to comment on how the writer has conveyed ideas about the pain of loss.

AIMING HIGH

Don't be afraid to give your view of a poem's meaning and how its effects are achieved. Originality of interpretation is seen as a higher skill, provided it answers the question and you offer clear evidence.

> 'Have you news of my boy Jack?'
> Not this tide.
> 'When d'you think that he'll come back?'
> Not with this wind blowing, and this tide.
> 5 'Has anyone else had word of him?'
> Not this tide.
> For what is sunk will hardly swim,
> Not with this wind blowing and this tide.
> 'Oh, dear, what comfort can I find?'
> 10 None this tide,
> Nor any tide,
> Except he did not shame his kind-
> Not even with that wind blowing, and that tide.
> Then hold your head up all the more,
> 15 This tide,
> And every tide;
> Because he was the son you bore,
> And gave to that wind blowing and that tide!

- The story or subject of the poem: this is a poem about trying to find answers to loss and grief
- Tone: the poem is sad, questioning what has happened to Kipling's son, what that means and what the poetic voice's role was in that loss
- Most notable features: a series of questions are posed and then answered with a repeated line, which is altered as the poet's ideas develop. Probably the reason for no stanzas

SECOND READING

Next working from your initial notes, dig deeper into the poem. In this case, the most outstanding features are structural, so start with those.

❶ What is the effect of the repeated rhetorical questions in lines 1, 3, 5 and 10?

(Note that: The answers to these questions are developed through the poem from 'Not this tide' in the second line, to 'And gave to that wind blowing and that tide!' in the last line.)

❷ What is the effect of the developed repetition in these answers?

(Note that: The poem is not divided into stanzas, reflecting the endless nature of the questioning, but it does have a rhyming pattern with a strong feature being the CBBC pattern in lines 9–12.)

❸ What is the effect of having this rhyming pattern in the middle of the poem?

AIMING HIGH ⭐

Look for opportunities to comment on less 'flashy' language choices made by the writer as these can be just as effective. For example, the determiner 'this' (wind and tide) is contrasted with 'that' as the poem progresses – contrasting the current and future time with the past (what cannot be changed).

APPLYING YOUR SKILLS (A02)

❹ Consider the use of language in the poem, in particular the metaphor of the wind and tide. How is language used to create meaning and tone in relaying a sense of loss?

PROGRESS CHECK FOR CHAPTER FIVE ✓

GOOD PROGRESS

I can:
- I can understand the main focuses exam questions ☐
- I can approach unseen passages and poems with confidence ☐

EXCELLENT PROGRESS

I can:
- I can confidently identify the key focus of exam questions and plan a sophisticated response ☐
- I can analyse unseen passages and poems confidently and effectively with a developed response ☐

INTRODUCTION: PUTTING IT INTO PRACTICE

This is an opportunity to put all your skills into practice by applying them to some reading questions based on the type you will meet in your exams. Before you start, remember the following:

- **Read the questions carefully**, decoding them and identifying the content and process words
- Look at the **number of marks allocated** to each question as this provides an indication of the length and detail required in the answer
- **Read the extracts through twice if possible**, once for general meaning and tone, and a second, more detailed reading, keeping in mind the question being asked
- **Annotate** as you read the passages
- For the longer answers, **make a plan and refer to it** as you answer the question, ticking each point off as you go and crossing it through at the end to show it is not part of your answer
- **Check back through your work** at the end for legibility and accuracy

PAPER 1 READING (FICTION)

TEXT A

This is an extract from *The Hound of the Baskervilles* by Sir Arthur Conan Doyle, and comes at the plot **climax** towards the end of the novel, Holmes and Watson, the two detectives investigating the murder of Sir Charles Baskerville, are lying in wait for the hound who is in pursuit of the inheritor of the Baskerville estate, Sir Henry.

> *A sound of quick steps broke the silence of the moor. Crouching among the stones we stared intently at the silver-tipped bank in front of us. The steps grew louder, and through the fog, as through a curtain, there stepped the man whom we were awaiting. He*
> 5 *looked round him in surprise as he emerged into the clear, starlit night. Then he came swiftly along the path, passed close to where we lay, and went on up the long slope behind us. As he walked he glanced continually over either shoulder, like a man who is ill at ease.*
> 10 *'Hist!' cried Holmes, and I heard the sharp click of a cocking pistol. 'Look out! It's coming!'*
> *There was a thin, crisp, continuous patter from somewhere in the heart of that crawling bank. The cloud was within fifty yards of where we lay, and we glared at it, all three, uncertain what horror*
> 15 *was about to break from the heart of it. I was at Holmes's elbow, and I glanced for an instant at his face. It was pale and exultant, his eyes shining brightly in the moonlight. But suddenly they started forward in a rigid, fixed stare, and his lips parted in amazement.*

20 *At the same instant Lestrade gave a yell of terror and threw himself face downward upon the ground. I sprang to my feet, my inert hand grasping my pistol, my mind paralysed by the dreadful shape which had sprung out upon us from the shadows of the fog. A hound it was, an enormous coal-black hound, but not such a hound as mortal eyes have ever seen. Fire burst from its open mouth, its*

25 *eyes glowed with a smouldering glare, its muzzle and hackles and dewlap[1] were outlined in flickering flame. Never in the delirious dream of a disordered brain could anything more savage, more appalling, more hellish, be conceived than that dark form and savage face which broke upon us out of the wall of fog.*

30 *With long bounds the huge creature was leaping down the track, following hard upon the footsteps of our friend. So paralysed were we by the apparition that we allowed him to pass before we had recovered our nerve. Then Holmes and I both fired together, and the creature gave a hideous howl, which showed that one at*

35 *least had hit him. He did not pause, however, but bounded onwards. Far away on the path we saw Sir Henry looking back, his face white in the moonlight, his hands raised in horror, glaring helplessly at the frightful thing which was hunting him down.*

But that cry of pain from the hound had blown all our fears to

40 *the winds. If he was vulnerable he was mortal, and if we could wound him we could kill him. Never have I seen a man run as Holmes ran that night. I am reckoned fleet of foot, but he outpaced me as much as I outpaced the little professional. In front of us as we flew up the track we heard scream after scream from Sir Henry and*

45 *the deep roar of the hound. I was in time to see the beast spring upon its victim, hurl him to the ground and worry at his throat. But the next instant Homes had emptied five barrels of his revolver into the creature's flank. With a last howl of agony and a vicious snap in the air, it rolled upon its back, four feet pawing furiously, and then*

50 *fell limp upon its side. I stooped, panting, and pressed my pistol to the dreadful, shimmering head, but it was useless to press the trigger. The giant hound was dead.*

Glossary:
[1] *dewlap* – a loose fold of skin hanging from beneath the throat

Q1 Read again the first part of the source from **lines 1 to 9,** 'A sound of quick steps' to 'like a man who is ill at ease'.

List four things from this part of the text about the man, Sir Henry Baskerville.

[4 marks]

Q2 Read **lines 22 to 31,** 'A hound it was' to 'hard upon the footsteps of our friend'.

How does the writer describe the hound in these lines?

You could include the writer's choice of:

- words and phrases
- language features and techniques
- sentence forms

You must refer to the text to support your answer.

Q3 You now need to think about the whole of the source. The extract is from the climax of the plot, near the end of the novel.

How has the writer structured the text to interest you as a reader?

You could write about:

- What the writer focuses your attention on at the beginning
- How and why the writer changes this focus as the source develops
- Any other structural features that interest you

[8 marks]

Q4 From **line 31 to the end,** 'So paralysed were we by the apparition' to 'the giant hound was dead.', the writer encourages the reader to feel a strong sense of tension and fear. To what extent do you agree with this view?

You should write about:

- Your own impressions of tension and fear as it is presented here and in the passage as a whole
- How the writer has created these impressions

[20 marks]

PAPER 2 READING (NON-FICTION)

TEXT A

Letting developers vandalise the countryside won't solve the housing crisis

Nick Herbert, *The Guardian*, 14 July 2013 (theguardian.com)
Copyright Guardian News & Media Ltd 2017

Shakespeare knew it, when he gave 'this sceptered isle' to John of Gaunt's[1] dying breath. Great artists knew it when they took their easels to the summit of our hills and captured England's finest landscapes. Soldiers knew it, when wartime propaganda urged victory to protect the countryside we love. The London Olympic designers knew it, when their
5 *opening ceremony defined our modern nation with pastoral scenes. [...] even the government knows it. New official posters promoting Britain remind tourists that our 'countryside is great'.*

Everyone knows it. The countryside is integral to the definition of Britain. It is indelibly part our heritage. It is a national asset that should be prized. So why are we so criminally
10 *casual about its loss?*

The vandalism of rural Britain isn't happening with ordered precision. Each year, an area of countryside the size of Southampton is covered with concrete. But we aren't building inspiring new towns or green cities.

No, this loss is horribly random. Dismal, identikit developments disfigure historic market
15 *towns. Precious green spaces between villages are thoughtlessly destroyed. We are told not to worry, that only a few percentage points of countryside will be lost. The reality is that, outside of protected landscapes like national parks, the effective ruination of countryside and tranquillity is far greater.*

It's not just beauty that is sacrificed for careless construction. Villages expand, yet their
20 *shops and pubs disappear. As the heart of historic market towns slowly stops beating, anonymous drive-throughs and cloned chains on out-of-town retail parks turn communities inside out.*

England saw once before what random development would mean for the countryside. The great construction of the 1930s, which created millions of new homes, finally alarmed
25 *politicians when they saw that the suburban sprawl would not stop. The Town and Country Planning Act 1947 was brought in to end the era of unplanned development.*

Ministers invoke that halcyon[2] period of housing boom as an easy route once again out of recession, yet they forget the emergency action that followed. And that was in an era before mass ownership of cars. Today, simply relaxing planning controls wouldn't just see
30 *creeping suburbia: it would allow random development on any countryside that someone would sell.*

Yes, planning controls drive up prices; yes, we once again have a housing shortage, and, yes, homes have never been so unaffordable. We do need to lower prices and rents. We should want to extend opportunity and enable young people to realise their dreams of
35 *ownership.*

But this requires fundamental planning reform, not ill-thought relaxation of controls that were introduced for good reason. [...]

Glossary:
[1] *this sceptred isle* – quotation describing Britain from Shakespeare's *King Richard II*
[2] *halcyon* – idyllically happy and peaceful time from the past

TEXT B

Extract from *The Rural Life of England* by William Howitt, 1838.

Lancashire is famous for its immense manufactures, and consequent immense population. In ranging over its wild, bleak hills, we are presently made sensible of the vast difference between the character and habits of the working class, and the character and
5 *habits of the pastoral and agricultural districts. We have no longer those picturesque villages and cottages half buried in their garden and orchard trees; no longer those home-crofts, with their old, tall hedges; no longer rows of bee-hives beneath their little thatched southern sheds; those rich fields and farm-houses, surrounded with*
10 *wealth of corn-ricks, and herds and flocks. You have no longer that quiet and Arcadian-looking¹ population; hedgers and ditchers, ploughmen and substantial farmers, who seem to keep through life the 'peaceful tenor of their way', in old English fulness and content. There may indeed, and there are, such people scattered here and*
15 *there; but they and their abodes are not of the class which gives the predominant character to the scenery. On the contrary, everywhere extend wild naked hills, in many places totally unreclaimed; in others, enclosed, but exhibiting all the signs of a neglected and spiritless husbandry; with stunted fences or stone walls, and field*
20 *sodden with wet from want of drainage, and consequently over-grown with rushes. Over those naked and desolate hills are scattered to their very tops, in all directions, the habitations of a swarming population of weavers; the people and their homes equally unparticpant of those features which delight the poet and*
25 *the painter. The houses are erections of stone or brick, covered with glaring red tiles, as free from any attempt at beauty or ornament as possible. Without, where they have gardens, those gardens are as miserable and neglected as the fields; within, they are squalid and comfortless.*

Glossary:
¹ *Arcadian-looking* – Arcadia is the idealised countryside setting of Classical poetry, and represents a quiet, simple rural life

Q1 Refer to Text A:

a) Name **one** person or persons inspired by the British countryside.

b) Identify **one** negative effect that planning controls have.

[2 marks]

Q2 Refer to Text B:

a) Name **one** thing that Lancashire is well-known for.

b) Identify **any two** of the endangered rural occupations mentioned by the writer.

[2 marks]

Q3 Refer to both texts. According to these two writers what do they fear losing from the **villages** as the result of increased urbanisation?

[8 marks]

Q4 Refer only to Text A.

How does Nick Herbert use language to make the reader feel that urbanisation is a bad thing?

[12 marks]

Q5 Both these texts suggest that the countryside was better in the past.

Compare the following:

- The writers' attitudes towards the past
- The methods they use to get across their views or experiences

You must use the text to support your comments and make it clear which text you are referring to

[16 marks]

ANSWERS

CHAPTER 1

1.1 Understanding genre and form [pp. 5–7]

1 Text types: Extract A – Persuasive speech; Extract B – Novel; Extract C – Formal letter; Extract D – Magazine article

2 The extract is from a travel magazine article and uses literary techniques such as personification, 'sugar cane waved tasselled heads' and alliteration 'life slowed to the laid-back languor' to create a vivid picture of the island. The inclusion of personal experience 'we were embraced by the warm air' makes the destination appealing to the reader.

1.2 Identifying the purpose and theme [pp. 8–9]

1 The details create a vivid set of memories which older readers might relate to; the reference to the missing 'tin-opener' causing an arguments is comical.

2 Core ideas: A = Robots now have the skills to do certain jobs instead of humans; B = New airline has potential to fly in the upper stratosphere/great economic potential; C = Whether or not teenagers are ready for the responsibility of voting.

3 The core idea is that High Streets are in serious decline.

The purpose of the piece is to raise awareness of the decline of traditional town centres.

1.3 Understanding audience and reader [pp. 10–11]

1 1 = B; 2 = A; 3 = C

2 Changes to school security systems – formal, using mixture of fact and opinion; The difficulty of children's homework – chatty, using personal experience and quotations, informal and engaging; Review – Harry Potter and the Cursed Child – clear and direct, entertaining and informative.

3 Because he was writing for the rightful king of the day, he didn't want people to think a king like that could be removed so easily.

4 Because rebellion and the overthrow of kings and queens was a reality they would have known about.

5 Sample paragraph: This magazine article is aimed at people who are wanting to lose weight after Christmas. It is aimed at a general audience, both men and women, who could be any age but who are interested in maintaining a healthy weight as suggested by the advice to keep 'a food diary' and

conduct a 'comprehensive examination of what you eat and drink' rather than follow 'food fads'. These details might also imply an audience who have tried diets and not been completely successful before.

1.4 Facts, statistics and opinions [pp. 12–13]

1 Only the last penultimate sentence contain statistics; the rest contain facts.

2 Left-hand column: first two entries are facts; second two entries contain statistics

Right-hand column: first and third entries contain clear statistics; second is a fact; fourth entry has a statistic but it is rather vague ('millions' rather than a specific figure)

3 Answers to remaining annotations: 2 opinion/ assertion; 3 opinion; 4 statistic; 7 opinion; 8 opinion ; 10 fact; 11 opinion; 12 fact; 13 opinion/assertion.

4 The article doesn't really present a balanced view but a biased one as there is nothing negative included. The mention of average temperatures of 18 degrees, the availability of fruit, the beauty of the colours, and the Keats quotation all present autumn in a positive way.

5 Autumn is an awful time. Not only is it the end of the summer holidays, when temperatures start to fall, it is also the start of the school term. Days begin to shorten and evenings are darker, leading to a 20% rise in traffic accidents in our area. Trees begin to lose their leaves and the squelchy mulch underfoot is slippery and smelly. Even shorter days and colder weather are coming, and once all the leaves have fallen off the trees there will be no colour left. It is long time before the next summer holiday comes round.

1.5 Character and voice [pp. 14–17]

1 Three explicit details from the following: Mrs Joe has black hair and eyes; her skin is rather red; she is tall and bony; she wore her apron a lot; she had pins stuck into it.

2 The description of the apron shows that Mrs Joe spends a lot of her time doing domestic work and that she resents the fact 'that she wore this apron so much'. The bib of the apron is described as being 'impregnable' and 'stuck full of pins and needles' which suggest her domestic role is a barrier to love and affection.

3 Tone of narrative voice in the *Great Expectations* extract: is critical of Mrs Joe but also sad and thoughtful as 'Pip' reflects on his sister; also a touch comical in its detail.

4 *Pride and Prejudice* has an omniscient narrator; *The Curious Incident of the Dog in the Night time* has a first person narrator.

5 We are told, by the narrator, that Mr Bennet has an ironic sense of humour but is distanced, whilst Mrs Bennet isn't very intelligent and is rather foolish.

The narrator of *The Curious Incident* has a particular view of the world, demonstrated by his comments on what makes a good day, and he has some psychiatric issues, as he is seeing a psychologist.

1.6 Language and style [pp.18–19]

1 They create a vivid picture of sickly looking skin and unhealthy eyes which conveys a grotesque, frightening mood.

2 a) Both communicate similar information but the effect is very different. Extract A is factual, using concrete language to tell the reader directly about the bird. Extract B is descriptive, using more abstract language to convey the feeling and emotion of the bird's flight. **b)** Two examples of concrete language from A = 'large brown bird' and 'rounded wing-ends'; two examples of abstract language from B = 'soared effortlessly' and 'hapless small creatures'.

3 'screeched' is onomatopoeic; 'like dragon's breath' is a simile; 'screeched', 'scorching' and 'shrivelling' are alliterative, if a little far apart – the last two repeating a phrase pattern of '-ing' verbs.

4 Answers to remaining annotations: 3. Suggests danger through the onomatopoeia of the adders' hiss; 4. Conveys the exotic nature of the birds and their liveliness; 8. Simile suggests the mass of men and their movement; 9. Verb choice shows the destructive power of the movement; 11. Verbs contrast the violent actions with the delicacy of the nouns describing nature.

1.7 Understanding context [pp. 20–23]

1 Answers might include:

- The depiction of a very low wage, 'five-and-sixpence', as a 'bewildering income'.
- Martha's obvious fatigue at the long hours she would have worked as an apprentice milliner for very little money.
- The impression is of a family in which all have to contribute to make ends meet.

2 Answers will vary.

3 Her first response suggests that the normal attitude is to see young women as less than human, as simple fodder to service the factories, linking to the lack of social and political power women had at the time. Her second response suggests that well-off women at the time were protected from such abuse and therefore need to put themselves in the shoes of working-class girls more often.

4 a) The phrase 'could not be insensible to the compliments of such a man's affection' suggests that traditionally a woman would have been expected to welcome such a proposal from 'such a man.' The phrase 'answer with patience' suggests that it should be her role to be polite and courteous, whatever her personal feelings.

b) She wants to answer him 'in anger'; she also dislikes his assumption that she will welcome his proposal so is 'exasperated' and wants to let him know how she feels.

5 Harrison is a new immigrant from Africa and in order for his family to make the move, they have been split. There is a reflection of concerns about diseases being transmitted from abroad, but also an undercurrent of racism in Vilis's reaction to him.

CHAPTER 2

2.1 Using quotations and evidence [pp. 24–27]

1 Quotations, in addition to the examples given, could include: 'a wall of colour' and 'reaching far above our heads' (line 3);'showing no leaf, no twig, nothing' (lines 6-7)

2 and 3 Answers will vary.

4 a) Examples could include: 'There was something bewildering, even shocking' (line 4); 'The woods had not prepared me for them' (line 5); 'They startled me' (line 5); 'unlike any rhododendron plant I had ever seen before' (lines 7-8).

b) They suggest that Rebecca is disorientated, inexperienced and unprepared for what lies ahead.

5 a) Words that could replace 'hard' in 'hard journey': 'difficult'; 'challenging', 'tough', 'gruelling', 'demanding'.

b) The most suitable synonyms for 'warder' from the list are 'custodian' or 'gate-keeper'.

6 Model paraphrase: 'Early recollections of school meals are of being made to consume cheap, overcooked and unappetising food.'

7 a) Jane is overcome with emotion when talking to Rochester and cannot keep her feelings hidden, saying that she wished she 'had never been born' or 'come to Thornfield'.

b) She feels strongly about Thornfield as she cries violently and trembles all over as she tries to speak.

2.2 Identifying explicit and implicit information [pp. 28–29]

1 The piano is new, it's a cottage piano, it was bought on credit, it was manufactured by W. Bilkson and from Collard and Collard.

2 The impression given is that George and Carrie might not have much to say to each other and that their relationship isn't close, revealed by 'can manage to pass' their evenings without company and spend that time busying themselves with tasks.

3 The words 'great comfort' suggest that they love their son and 'getting on so well' implies that they are proud of him. However, 'We should like to see more of him' suggests that they probably aren't that close to him.

4 We are told that the coastal areas are very diverse and range from historic resorts, to more remote, scenic beaches, including islands.

5 The suggestion is that the narrator doesn't appear to favour the traditional resorts very much, describing them negatively as 'tired', of being 'reduced' and of being 'beleaguered'.

2.3 Interpreting information [pp. 30–31]

1 'odious, stingy, hard, unfeeling'; 'Nobody knows it better than you'; 'My dear,' was Bob's mild answer,

'Christmas Day', suggesting that on this day of all days, people should forgive.

2 a) Mrs Cratchit raises the toast for her husband's sake; b) Mrs Cratchit doesn't think Scrooge will be very happy over Christmas and that this reflects badly on him as it is due to failings in his character. c) The children are also unenthusiastic about the toast, talk of Scrooge takes the pleasure out of things, but this could be a reflection of their mother's opinion of him.

3 Answer = b)

4 His clerk isn't very happy at work and has a good home-life that he wants to get back to. C: He doesn't attach much significance to Christmas and doesn't understand why others do. D: He's mean and considers money above most other things.

5 Answers will vary.

2.4 Summarising and synthesising ideas [pp. 32–33]

1 a) The daughter: seven years old; took 3 months to persuade father about dog; she had lots of 'tricks' to persuade him; she seemed to like all dogs she saw. b) The dog: it was a puppy; it was very naughty.

2 He'd grown up with dogs and enjoyed their friendship and affection; children learn how to look after other living beings.

3 The first father needs persuading by his 7-year-old daughter who uses lots of means to get him to agree to having one, whereas the second father is already convinced of the benefits of having a dog. His own experiences have shown him the affectionate and companionable side of dogs, and he also believes they help children learn responsibility.

4 The environment is dark, windy, snowy and bleak but the poetic voice seems compelled to stay.

CHAPTER 3

3.1 Writers' methods and effects [pp. 34–35]

1 a) Punctuation: question marks; a lot of sentences with commas to separate lists of ideas; dashes; exclamation marks; semi-colons.

b) Questions; emphatic statement; longer sentences made up of several clauses with exclamatory phrases within them.

2 Effects: a) all three usages suggest Jane's active,

intelligent mind, through her rhetorical questioning, exclamations which assert her strength of feeling, and dashes which show her adding ideas to build her passionate argument. b) Structure – it conveys Jane's emotion and the significance of the appeal she is making. c) Literary techniques – it builds passion in the piece and makes links between their respective positions in life.

3 Answers will vary.

4 a) Methods used: Narrative view – the passage is written from the woman's viewpoint.

Character and voice – she is angry and has lost some grip on reality but speaks in an educated voice and clearly has had a sense of proper behaviour.

Language and style – the language combines simple description, 'I tried to lift and push it', with more bizarre actions 'I bit off a little piece at one corner'. There is also a contrast between violent actions and a diminishing of their consequences, 'To jump out of the window would be admirable exercise' and her behaviour with her sense of what 'is improper'. The language for the description of the wallpaper is more complex, with words such as 'bulbous' and 'derision'.

Structure – there is a combination of short sentences conveying actions, with longer ones that offer explanations.

Literary techniques – the wallpaper is personified as if it is something malevolent, mocking her, 'the pattern just enjoys it! All those strangled heads and bulbous eyes and waddling fungus growths just shriek with derision!'.

b) Effects of methods: Narrative view – the woman's perspective offers an insight into her state of mind.

Character and voice – sympathy is created for her by the suggestion of how far her mind has altered.

Language and style – clearly reflects the woman's confused mental state.

Structure – the short sentences show the brutality of her actions whilst the longer sentences showing her own rationalisation demonstrates her disturbed state of mind.

Literary techniques – the description of the wall paper generates pity for a mind that misconstrues something harmless as something unpleasant and unkind.

3.2 Vocabulary for effect [pp. 36–38]

1 Answers will vary.

2 B is the more informal in style of the two texts. Vocabulary choices indicating this include:'Hi', 'Cheers', 'gutted', 'cool', 'workmate'.

3 The technical vocabulary in the extract, such as 'fixed focus lens', 'telephoto' and 'focal length', relates to photography. This, together with the woman's efficient actions, suggests she is a skilled, professional photographer.

4 The emotive words in the paragraph are 'utterly bored', 'longed for', 'freedom' and 'miserable'. The first three show the sad effects of captivity on the lions and the last reflects the emotional response of the photographer to their misery.

5 It is colloquial, informal language, which might suggest a lack of education (non-standard English) or simply the language Terry shares with his friends when chatting.

6 Sample paragraph: From Harrison's choice of vocabulary, it is clear he is a keen observer but that English is not his first language. His use of 'Asweh' rather than 'I swear' reflects his accent, and his mistake in the idiom 'donkey hours' instead of 'donkey's years' shows that English is still a little unfamiliar to him. Words like 'thiefman' (instead of 'burglar') and sentences like 'Asbo did a big sneeze.' (instead of 'Asbo sneezed loudly.') may reflect words and sentence constructions from his first language. However, his knowledge of other words such as Asbo show he is assimilating into his community.

7 Answers to remaining annotations: 3 Unrelenting – another powerful word choice suggesting continued pressure, the effect of which is highlighted by substituting the word for the more ambivalent 'constant'; 4 Vulnerable –an example of emotive language that suggests a particular weakness that is communicated less in a substituted word such as 'unprotected'; Entitled –a formal use of language which is highlighted by substituting the more everyday choice of 'allowed'; 6 Nervous-breakdown- this is a **colloquial**, emotive use of language which suggests a lack of ordinary common sense that is highlighted by substituting it with a more objective word such as 'malfunction'.

8 a) Significance of differences: 'Through' suggests a movement through to the other side, whereas 'from' suggests fleeing or escaping; second line which shows the desperation of the charge, is omitted entirely to mute that feeling, and the last line omits 'Russian' to make the foe more generalised.

b) Answers will vary.

3.3 Sentences for impact and meaning [pp. 39–40]

1 a) The short sentence makes the reader pause too. **b)** The previous sentence is one of noise, energy and action, so this creates a dramatic contrast, cutting things off to try to work out what is going on.

2 The use of rhetorical questions engages the reader, addressing them directly and inviting their active participation.

3 Green highlight shows simple sentences; yellow highlight shows compound sentences; blue highlight shows complex sentences.

Sample paragraph: The writer uses short sentences to build tension and give a sense of key actions happening quickly with a rhetorical question to engage the reader at a key point in the narrative. Compound sentences are used to suggest contrast and speed as the events develop while the complex sentences add information at key points (separated off by a comma or a pair of commas), pausing the action momentarily or easing the tension.

3.4 Paragraphs and organisation [pp. 41–43]

1 A new paragraph has been started due to a change in time and location.

2 Changing the order of the two paragraphs would reduce the tension caused by the current order.

3 The short paragraph is a structural recreation of the surprise the narrator feels. The reader is halted, as a reader, just as the narrator is halted in the narrative.

4 The paragraph is about a pigeon being killed at a busy railway station by a Sparrow Hawk.

5 In the first example, the death of the pigeon comes first but the reader is not told who the culprit is until the final sentence. Withholding this information from the reader creates the suspense.

In the second paragraph, the reader is told that the Sparrow Hawk has killed straight away, but is not told the identity of the victim until the middle, and the lack of reaction from the commuters until the end, creating a different kind of tension.

6 The key information – that the narrator 'didn't see' his attacker – is foregrounded. Also, we don't know who 'him' is, or why it is important that he wasn't seen, so it creates tension and mystery. The sentences that follow provide explanation and express regret, but the first sentence is the one that grabs our attention.

7 Answers will vary.

8 Answers will vary.

3.5 Imagery and other literary techniques [pp. 44–45]

1 The repetition of the 'r' sounds like the firing of a machine gun.

2 The two onomatopoeic words in the second line are 'stuttering' and 'rattle'.

3 The alliteration in and the onomatopoeic use of 'winnowing' suggest of the sound of the gentle breeze, emphasising the sense of harmony and slowing the pace still further

4 Possible paragraph: The metaphor for the rain, which is likened to 'steel stair-rods', suggests its harshness and ferocity. The alliteration of 'dusty dry dirt' emphasises the contrast between conditions before the rain and the present, whilst the onomatopoeic use of 'plopping' makes the description of the aftermath on the car users more vivid. The presentation of the rain as a generous maternal gift, portrays it as a good thing that will

benefit the receivers.

3.6 Poetic style and structures [pp. 46–49]

1 It is less 'complete' and so it creates a less harmonious effect.

2 'Of <u>all</u> men <u>else</u> I <u>have</u> a<u>void</u>ed <u>thee</u>,

But <u>get</u> thee <u>back</u>, my <u>soul</u> is <u>too</u> much <u>charged</u>'

The stressed words suggest the danger of this encounter.

2 The poet sets up the initial internal rhymes in line 1 with 'high' and 'cry' to show the frightening sound of the hyena. This is echoed in the rhymes in lines 3 and 4 between 'lies',' 'light' and flies', which extend the sense of fear through the poem.

3 The stressed syllables in the second line put emphasis on 'fair Verona' as the main setting ('scene') for the action, making it plain to the audience that the drama will have a romantic location.

4 Subject and tone: the poem is about an illicit lovers' encounter.

Rhyme scheme is ABCCBA DEFFED with the second half of both stanzas mirroring the first half, like reflections in water. The pattern of the rhyme emphasises the middle lines, which in the first stanza highlights the **personification** of the waves, an image of a woman waking, that anticipates through the **structure** the actual awakening in the second stanza, caught in the intimacy of 'a lighted match'.

There are a number of examples of **alliteration** which create various effects: the repeated 'l' in the first two lines gives a languid feel that contrasts with the 'startled little waves'; the repetition of 'p' and 's' in lines 5 and 6 suggests a rhythmic movement; and the 's' in line 7 links the sea and the land and in line 10 emphasises the furtive lighting of the match.

5. a) Enjambment has been used between lines 1 and 2 and 2 and 3. In lines 1 and 2, this separates the powerful image of the hyena's cry and places the strong verb 'Echoes' at the start of a new line.

b) The two complete sentences are in lines 1–3 and line 4.

3.7 Dramatic style and structure [pp. 50–51]

1 a) Sheila's had some involvement in the events leading up to the girl's death; b) She is very affected by what she sees and feels compelled to leave – cannot trust her reactions in front of others

2 Eric's initial enthusiasm to agree, his check and his subsequent confusion, suggest that he knows more about women than his father thinks or he wants his father to realise.

3 a) They suggest that Sheila has the foresight to suspect that Gerald will also be implicated in the young woman's death. It also suggests that Gerald knows what is likely to happen and is struggling to remain in control of himself. **b)** The Inspector's control is conveyed by his directness and his need to use very few words to prompt a response first from Sheila and then from Gerald. His 'Well?' flusters the near 'hysterical' Shelia and then he turns straight to Gerald for his account of how he knew the dead woman.

3.8 Evaluating texts [pp.52–53]

1. Answers will vary.

2 a) The first sentence suggests that, in her husband's view, Carrie is not physically very strong and that he takes pleasure in seeing her eat well at the dinner. This could be seen as a rather sexist view of women as delicate creatures from the male perspective.

b) Charles appears to be disappointed that his ironmonger has also been invited to the civic dinner.

He says it is to his 'amazement' that he turns to meet Farmerson. And he is not pleased to be greeted in 'the most familiar way' by someone he considers his social inferior. He responds 'coolly', making it clear that he thinks the ironmonger is out of place.

3 Possible response: The sense of tension and menace is generated successfully in several ways as the extract unfolds. The description of the bell sounding like 'someone laughing hysterically' is rather unnerving to begin with and is supported by the 'gloomy' and 'damp' aspects of the hallway'. The menacing effect of these sensory images is then reflected in the narrator's own fear as finds himself 'stammering' with his opening words 'I'm, I'm looking...' The dialogue continues to generate a sense of menace with the phrase 'and there's no forwarding address', suggesting the former lodger has mysteriously disappeared, coupled with the eerie tone of the speaker's voice which is 'strangely quiet'.

CHAPTER 4

4.1 What is comparison? [pp. 54–55]

1 Possible response: Writer A is very positive about Christmas, with heart-warming images of gathering together and joining in song, whereas writer B presents a more negative perspective on Christmas, thinking about the pressures of getting together as a family for a period of time.

2 The best words to support the student's points: A = 'draw nearer the blazing fire', 'fill the glass' and joining in 'song'; B = 'Tensions' and 'buried beneath the mound [...] forced to the surface'.

3 Possible response: The imagery of 'blazing fire', 'fill the glass and send round the song' creates a picture of family and friends gathered together in warmth and harmony, sharing refreshment and entertainment. In contrast, the extended metaphor of 'Tensions' that are usually 'buried beneath the mound' of everyday life being 'forced to the surface' by a family being together in one place for Christmas sounds like a natural disaster waiting to happen. It creates a sense of strife and destructive energy.

4 Possible response: Both extracts are about the difficulties of the festive season but Source A appeals to the reader to make the best of things whereas Source B reports the problems. Source A has a resolutely cheerful tone whereas Source B has a tone of weary resignation. Both pieces address the image of Christmas as a family time for celebrating, but

Source A suggests it as a reality, 'look at the merry faces of your children', whereas Source B suggests it is a facade, 'a haze of bonhomie and Christmas jumpers'. In Source A the writer addresses the reader directly, 'thank God it's no worse', engaging and inviting them to consider their own family and circumstances whereas in Source B the focus is more general and distanced, 'Tensions, buried beneath the bustle of school, work and geographical distance'. Source A is more emotive, evoking stoicism, with phrases such as, 'thank God it's no worse', and 'one little seat may be empty'. Source B is more factual, listing the potential issues: 'marital stresses, financial constraints, sibling rivalries and over-indulgence'. Whilst both sources acknowledge there are difficulties associated with Christmas, Source A recommends stoicism, 'put a brave face on the matter', whereas Source B reveals some bleak facts, 'There is a reason that lawyers nickname the first working Monday after the Christmas break, "Divorce Day"'.

4.2 Analysing language for comparison [pp. 56–59]

1 a) The writer's viewpoint is against child labour where this means children are bound to work long hours ('incessant labours') cooped up in factories in dangerous ('gas and steam') and harsh conditions ('severe punishment') for very little reward.

b) Evidence from the passage for the view that child labour dehumanises children includes: 'reduces the Child [...] to the rank of an animal machine [...] a breathing automaton'; like an animal they are subject to 'broken rest, severe punishment, excessive toil.'

2 Two further words or phrases showing what the child labourers miss out on: 'forest wave', 'streams run glittering in the light'.

3 Answers will vary.

4 Answers will vary.

5 Answer = c)

6 Completed paragraph: The writer feels that the factory system has a terrible impact on children's humanity, making them an 'animal machine' or a 'breathing automaton'. The metaphor suggests that they become part of the factory as if swallowed up by it. Because of this, they will miss out on the pleasures of nature and fresh air, where the sun shines, the colourful 'flowers bloom', 'forest wave' and 'streams run glittering in the light'. To add to this, they will be denied rest and the best 'viands', other necessities for humanity to thrive.

7 The two repeated words are 'the only'.

8 While the summary is accurate in summing up the tone of the extract about child labour, it could mention how the writer's use of language is particularly emotive and affecting when he draws the contrast between factory life and the natural world.

9 Possible response: The adjectives 'bright', 'shiny', 'new' and 'dazzling' convey a sense of vivid modernity. The repeated trio of negatives at the end also emphasise the clean, functional nature of the factory.

10 The different viewpoints expressed with evidence

Extract A:

The calamity of the fire: 'God grant mine eyes may never behold the like'

The sheer extent of the fire: 'All sky was a fiery aspect [...] seen above 40 miles round about for many nights'; '10,000 houses all in one flame'

The damage done to the city and community: 'the fall of towers, houses, churches'

The comparison with mythical burning of Troy and the biblical fires of Sodom

Extract B:

The Lewes bonfire: as a commemoration and 'a celebration, not destruction'

Preparations for the event: raising money, making costumes

Procession through the streets to music – 'march proudly through the streets'

Ceremony of throwing the flaming pole onto the fire – a symbol of 'local pride and local unity'

11 Possible response: Evelyn uses adjectives such as 'miserable', 'calamitous' and 'hideous' which convey the destructive, ugly effect of the fire. He also uses a simile to describe the fire in the sky, 'like the top of a burning oven', suggesting the wall of flame and smoke. The imagery of the 'cracking' and 'thunder' gives a vivid aural sense of the fire's effects. Later, he uses biblical and classical analogies to Sodom, a sinful city, and Troy, a great city destroyed in battle, which add to the sense of this being a momentous event. The long third sentence creates a sense of the disaster building up; the final short sentence is a grim and to-the-point summary.

Gould's account is much more positive. He uses the word 'celebration', which suggests a joyful community event, backed up by nouns such as 'pride' and 'unity.' The description of the actual events creates an exciting tone with participants who 'march proudly' and are 'swept along'. Visual and aural imagery builds a sense of a colourful, uplifting spectacle in the 'flaming crosses' which warm revellers, and the 'lively music' which accompanies them. The final sentence uses rhetorical power in the three noun phrases beginning 'local', which emphasise the spirit of community.

4.3 Comparing poems [pp. 60–63]

1 Overall impressions of the poets' attitudes to Nature: In Poem A, Hardy presents a gloomy and despondent view of nature where the landscape and animals that live in it are downhearted and lacking in vitality. It is as if they have been left unsupported by the God that made them. In contrast, in Poem B Manley Hopkins portrays Nature as vibrant and colourful. The variety and contrariness of nature is all brought about by God whom Hopkins thanks for this.

2 Answers will vary.

3 Possible response: In Poem A, the poet seems to present a slightly forlorn view of Nature. With its 'field, flock and lonely tree' the reader gets a sense of a landscape that has been left untended or uncared for. In comparison, the countryside of Poem B is all planned out, 'plotted and pieced – fold, fallow and plough' as if part of a more harmonious, well-tended estate.

4 For the comparison, you might have picked out some of the following points:

The final stanzas of both poems tackle religious uncertainty, but in the Hardy poem it is negative 'No answerer I...' whereas in the Hopkins' poem it is celebratory 'Praise him'.

Hardy's poem uses assonance, 'old glooms', to slow the pace and linger on the image of earth personified as an old person, and alliteration in the final words 'neighbours nigh' contributing to the negativity, whereas Hopkins uses alliteration to emphasise the positivity of contrasts, listing opposites, 'swift, slow; sweet, sour', separated by semi-colons, to emphasise the pairings and ending in, 'Praise Him', which links with the hymn –like opening.

Hardy's poem uses ellipses to create a sense of uncertainty in the final stanza, which is one long sentence, whereas Hopkins punctuates heavily and confidently underlining the certainty of the final stanza. He also uses a dash between 'fathers-forth' suggesting the onward, stable nature of God. The rhyming couplet at the end of Hopkins' final stanza, suggests certainty whereas the final line of Hardy's stanza is unrhymed suggesting unanswered questions.

CHAPTER 5

5.1 Decoding the question [pp. 64–65]

1 Answers to remaining annotations: 7. Content; 8. Process; 9. Content; 10. Process

2 Starting with the above speech [1], explain [2] how Shakespeare presents attitudes towards women in this play. [3]

Write about:
- What [4] is said about women in this speech [5]
- How Shakespeare presents [6] attitudes towards women in the play as a whole. [7]

Answers to annotations: 1. Content; 2. Process; 3. Content; 4. Process; 5. Content; 6. Process; 7. Content

5.2 Reading unseen passages [pp. 66–67]

1 Other factors about the environment described: it is windy; there are rocks beyond the trees and then the moorland.

2 Answers to annotations: 3. alliteration – emphasises negative aspects of the surroundings and Dr Watson's disturbed night; 4. strong, negative adjectives used linked to death and sadness; 5. A mixture of short and long sentences building tension; 6. description appealing to different senses, especially sight and sound, making it vivid.

5.3 Reading unseen poems [pp. 68–69]

1 The repeated rhetorical questions suggest the endless, troubled searching for answers. Together with their answers, they also evoke the ebb and flow of the tide.

2 The developed repetition suggests at first that there is no answer now, but by the middle of the poem, this has changed to never in 'Not any tide'. The final repetition and 'gave' in the last line implies an element of sacrifice.

3 It emphasises the movement towards the finality of 'Nor any tide' but also strongly connects the search for comfort with 'Except he did not shame his kind' suggesting the significance of the fact that honour was maintained.

4 Sample paragraph: 'This wind blowing, and this tide' create a specific storm metaphor that suggests the trauma of war and its elemental, relentless nature. The suggestion of 'what is sunk will hardly swim', emphasised by the alliteration of the opposing words 'sunk' and 'swim' is an acknowledgement of Jack's probable fate, which contrasts movingly with the intimacy of the opening 'my boy Jack'. In the final section of the poem, the pride of 'hold your head up all the more' is reduced by the acknowledgement that the poetic voice 'gave' his son up to the wind and tide of war.

CHAPTER 6

6.1 Paper 1 Reading (Fiction) [pp. 70–72]

The following are sample responses to the exam-style questions in this unit.

Q1 Any four of the following details about the man (Baskerville) could be accepted. He is:
- surprised when he emerges from the fog.
- walking quickly
- wondering if he's being followed
- being watched by Holmes, Watson and Lestrade
- ill at ease

Q2 Ways in which the hound is described as a supernatural and terrifying include the following:
- The hound's physical appearance, described using strong words 'enormous' and 'savage'; conventional imagery 'coal-black hound' recognisable to the reader as signs of something terrifying.

- Suggestions that the beast is outside human experience: not seen by 'mortal eyes', 'delirious dream of a disordered brain', emphasised by alliteration, and the choice of the word, 'hellish'.
- Its almost mythical association with fire, emphasising its most frightening physical aspects: 'Fire burst from its open mouth', 'its eyes glowed', 'smouldering glare', 'outlined in flickering flame'. Also the way this complex sentence build up these details in clauses.
- The listing of the adverbial clauses 'more savage, more appalling, more hellish'.

Q3 How the text is structured to interest the reader could include:

- At the beginning, through the tension of waiting for the man and then for the dog,
- The use of sensory description: 'quick steps', and, 'sharp click of a cocking pistol'
- Tension in the description of characters, for example, Sir Henry, who, 'glanced continually over either shoulder'.

Changing the focus from the man; to Holmes, Watson and Lestrade; and then to the dog.

- Shifts of pace through the use of short and long sentences and action scenes.

Q4 How the strong sense of tension and fear is constructed in the text could include the following:

In this section of the extract:

- The hound is so hideous the characters are, 'paralysed' with fear.
- The fact that even though the hound is hit and gives a, 'hideous howl', a powerful, alliterative and onomatopoeic use of language, he still continues his pursuit.
- Sir Henry's reaction, described in a series of strong images, 'face white', and, 'hands raised in horror', together with his, 'scream after scream'.
- Violence of the dog's attack depicted through strong verbs: 'spring', 'hurl', and, 'worry'.
- The detail that it took, 'five barrels', to kill it and it was struggling to the end.

In the extract as a whole:

- Use of the fog to generate a frightening atmosphere
- Several switches of focus
- Supernatural elements
- Fear in all the characters
- Changes in pace from slow waiting to action.

Mid Level extract: A clear and relevant evaluation, which uses a range of textual details to evaluate the effect(s) on the reader, e.g.

I agree that when I read this passage I feel a strong sense of tension and fear. It is very foggy and not being able to see clearly adds to the fear of what may be about to happen. In the extract the

characters are 'paralysed' by fear while the hound's movements are fast and furious: 'bounded', 'spring', 'hurl'. When Holmes and Watson burst after the hound the pace increases as does the fear and tension. As readers we see the reaction of Sir Henry and feel his fear. The writer does this through very strong language – his face is 'white' and his hands are lifted up in 'horror'. The writer also uses noises to alarm us before we see what is happening.

High Level extract: A perceptive and detailed evaluation using very well-chosen range of textual details to evaluate the effect(s) on the reader, e.g.

The writer uses many methods to encourage the reader to feel tension and fear. The semantic field of speed and impact is used to describe the movements of the hound which 'bound[s]' away and then 'spring[s] upon' his victim and 'hurl[s]' him to the ground. This contrasts with the paralysing fear that Holmes and Watson feel before they give chase. Sir Henry's reaction is described in a series of strong images – his 'white face', 'hands raised in horror' – which highlight his fear but also his vulnerability. The passage as a whole is enveloped in fog, and the writer cleverly uses this to add to the uncertainty and menace of the scene. The fact that we and the characters hear 'scream after scream' without knowing what has happened further intensifies the tension and fear.

6.2 Paper 2 Reading (Non-Fiction) [pp. 73–75]

The following are sample responses to the exam-style questions in this unit.

Q1 Any one of the following for individuals or groups inspired by the countryside: Shakespeare; artists; soldiers; the Olympic Park designers; the government.

Either of these negative effects: they drive up prices; they create a housing shortage.

Q2 Lancashire is famous for either of the following: large manufacturers; large populations.

Endangered rural occupations could be any two of the following: hedgers; ditchers; ploughmen; substantial farmers.

Q3 Nick Herbert fears the loss of shops and pubs from villages.

William Howitt fears losing cottages, home-crofts, tall hedges, bee hives, rich fields and farm houses, corn ricks, herds and flocks.

Q4 Nick Herbert's uses language to make the reader feel urbanisation is a bad thing with the following:

- examples from past and present e.g. Shakespeare and the Olympic Ceremony designers
- strong emotive language such as, 'indelibly part of our heritage', and, 'criminally casual'

facts introduced in an emotive way, e.g. 'area of countryside the size of Southampton' alliteration for emphasis, e.g. 'heart of historic', 'cloned chains', and, 'Dismal, identikit developments disfigure'

- personification to strengthen the sense of loss, e.g. 'As the heart of historic market towns slowly stops beating'
- answers to obvious counter-arguments, e.g. planning controls driving up property prices.

Q5 Both writers suggest that the countryside of the past was better as follows:

- Nick Herbert describes it as having a 'heart', absent from modern developments and William Hewitt describes it as conveying 'English fulness and content'.
- Both writers hark back to an historical view of the countryside quoting other sources, with Herbert referring to Shakespeare's image of, 'this sceptred isle', and Howitt the 'peaceful tenor of their way' (i.e. country dwellers).
- Both compare the appearance of modern dwellings unfavourably with those in the past with Herbert describing, 'Dismal, identikit developments', and Howitt houses, 'covered with glaring red tiles, as free from any attempt at beauty or ornament as possible'.
- Herbert uses strongly emotive, negative language and images, such as 'suburban sprawl', concentrating more on the present, whereas Howitt focuses on a, picture post-card view of an idyllic past, using romantic images of 'cottages half buried in their garden and orchards', contrasting these with the 'squalid and comfortless' gardens of new-style dwellings.

Mid Level extract: Ideas and perspectives are compared in clear and relevant way with reference to writers' methods, using relevant details, e.g.

Both writers see the countryside of the past as very important to them. Herbert quotes from Shakespeare to show this and describes how artists have 'captured' the landscape. Howitt compares the 'bleak' landscape with 'wild and naked hills' with what it was in the past, which was 'picturesque' and 'peaceful'. For Howitt the people are like insects – 'a swarming population' – which suggests that they have destroyed the landscape. Herbert also worries that today people are building new homes and destroying the countryside without understanding how important it is to Britain and that it is a 'national asset'.

High Level extract: Ideas and perspectives are compared perceptively by analysing writers' methods, with very well-chosen details from both texts, e.g.

Both writers use physical language to describe the intrinsic value of the countryside of the past – for Herbert it had a 'heart' while Howitt describes it as symbolising 'fulness and content'. Howitt takes this metaphor of the body further when he describes the industrial landscape as 'stunted', 'naked' and 'miserable'. This suggests that in destroying the countryside we are destroying ourselves and our peace of mind. In the same way, Herbert sees the countryside as part of what makes us British and suggests that with random, uncontrolled expansion, we not only lose green space but community spirit and a sense of 'tranquility'. Both writers use emotive language to describe the threat of the new situation – for Howitt the 'swarming population' has taken over, while for Herbert it is 'creeping surburbia' that he wants to fight. This contrasts with the peaceful picture-postcard view both writers present of the countryside of the past.

GLOSSARY

abstract noun a noun that refers to feelings, concepts, states that do not exist physically (e.g. hope, love)

accent the way in which a person pronounces words, often according to the region or country they come from.

adjective a word used to describe something or somebody (the *red* hat)

adverb used to modify a verb, adjective or another adverb, sometimes formed by adding 'ly' to an adjective

alliteration where the same sound is repeated in a stretch of language, usually at the beginning of words

anecdote a short amusing or interesting story about a real incident or person

antagonist the character that opposes or is the source of conflict and tension with the protagonist in a novel or story

assertion an unsubstantiated fact or belief

assonance when the same vowel sound appears in the same place in a series of words

bias tendency to promote one side of an argument topic or situation in a way considered to be unfair

blank verse verse written in unrhymed iambic pentameter often used by Shakespeare for his ordinary/menial characters

characterisation the process of portraying and developing a character in a novel, poem or play

chronological (order) the logical time order in which events take place

clause a phrase or group of words whose head is a verb. A clause can be a complete sentence.

climax the high point of the **narrative arc** in a play, act or story

colloquial the everyday style of speech used by people in ordinary situations

colon a punctuation mark (:) that precedes a list, or when a character speaks in a play script or an expansion in a sentence

complex sentence a sentence with a main clause and one or more subordinate clauses (e.g. 'Although he liked to read, he rarely did.')

compound sentence a sentence with two equal clauses joined by and, 'or' 'but' or 'so' (e.g. 'The dog would sit but would not lie down.')

concrete nouns a noun that refers to a material object that can be touched or seen.

conjunction a word that links two words or phrases together in a sentence to show the relationship between them, e.g. 'but', 'so' 'or'

connective a general term for words or phrases which link sentences or parts of sentences, e.g. 'and', 'while', 'furthermore', 'in the same way'

connotations meanings associated with a particular word, a thing or a concept (e.g. 'snow' = 'white', 'pure', 'cold')

consonance repeated consonant sounds within a sentence, paragraph or poem

context the social, literary or historical circumstances in which the text was written

conventions language or structural features of a particular type of text

dash a punctuation mark (—) used to set off a word or phrase after an independent clause

dialogue speech and conversation between characters

direct quotation words that are taken directly from a text or extract and which signalled by the use of inverted commas around them.

enjambment in poetry when a line runs on into the next line without pause, so carrying the though with it. Sometimes called a run-on line.

elegy a poem lamenting or mourning a death

ellipses a punctuation mark (...) that signals the omission of text or that more text should follow

explicit refers to information that is stated openly in a piece of writing

exposition the introduction of the setting, characters and situation early in the **narrative arc** in a story or a play

fact is something that can be proved to be true, usually by use of evidence

figurative non-literal and imaginative use of language, usually involving forms of imagery

first person the narrative perspective that uses 'I'

flashback a scene or part of a play, novel or film that goes back in time, prior to the main story

flashforwards a scene or part of a play, novel or film that goes forward in time, beyond the main story

form a type of writing with particular features

free verse a form of poetry; verses without regular rhythm or pattern, though they may contain some patterns, such as rhyme or repetition

genre a type of style of literary writing (e.g. a play, a novel, the Gothic, Fantasy writing, a ballad, a sonnet)

iambic pentameter a line of poetry consisting of five iambic feet (iambic consisting of a weak syllable followed by a strong one)

idiom typical phrases or expressions common to a language, e.g. you scared the living daylights out of me' meaning 'you scared me in the extreme'

imagery descriptive language that uses images to make actions, objects and characters more vivid in the reader's mind

implicit refers to information that is hinted at or suggested in a piece of writing

in media res when a story start in the middle of events

inference a conclusion based on evidence from a text

intensifiers used to increase a sense of a writer's emotion or viewpoint, often adverb-adjective combinations (e.g. 'really awful weather' or 'utterly divine decoration)

irony deliberately saying one thing when you mean another, usually in a humorous, sarcastic or sometimes thoughtful way

metaphor when one thing is used to describe another to create a striking or unusual image

minor characters characters that may only appear in parts of the text and interact with the protagonist and help to advance the story, e.g. Orlick, Drummle or Clara in *Great Expectations*. Also called secondary characters

mood the tone or atmosphere created by an artistic work

narrative arc the construction of the storyline in a novel or story from beginning through middle to end, though how it is told varies

narrator the character or voice telling a story; there may be multiple narrators in one text

nonfiction forms of writing, e.g. news articles, features, information texts, diaries, travel writing, that are based on fact or personal experience, not imagined or fictitious.

novella narrative **prose** longer than a short story, but shorter than a novel

omniscient narrator the voice in a novel or other work that is outside the story and appears to know everything and sound reliable

onomatopoeia a word that suggests its meaning through its sound (for example 'meow', 'squelch')

opinion is a belief, view or judgment about a topic that is not based on fact and which cannot be verified using evidence

pace the speed or rate at which a text or a performance moves

paragraph usually a series of sentences that have a common theme or topic, marked by starting a new line.

paraphrase a rewording of something written or spoken

personification the treatment or description of an object or idea as though they were human with human feelings and attributes

prose the natural flow of speech used in novels and other works and unlike poetry which has a more emphasised rhythmic structure

protagonist the main or a major character in a novel or story structure

purpose the reason for or aim of writing a text

refrain repeated lines or groups of words that convey the same meaning

register the choice of language used appropriate to social class or the particular context

repetition repeated words or patterns used for emphasis or a particular effect

resolution the end of the **narrative arc** in a play or story where things are uncovered, explained or resolved

rhetorical question asked for effect rather than for an answer

rhyme scheme the pattern of rhyme in a poem

rhyming couplet a couplet (two paired lines) that rhymes

rhythm the underlying beat of a poem often reinforced by the **rhyme scheme**

semantic field a set of vocabulary connected by a topic or subject, e.g. passion or football

semicolon a punctuation mark (;) which is used to link two ideas, events or pieces of information

sentence types there are three main sentence types: the **simple sentence** – with one main clause consisting of subject and a verb; the **compound sentence** – with two equal clauses joined by and, 'or' 'but' or 'so'; the **complex sentence** – with a main clause and one or more **subordinate clauses**

Shakespearean sonnet a sonnet that has an *abab cdcd efef gg* rhyme scheme. see also **sonnet**

simile when one thing is compared directly with another using 'like' or 'as'

simple sentence a sentence with one main clause consisting of subject and a verb, (e.g. The sun shone steadily…)

sonnet a fourteen-line verse with a rhyming couplet at the end

stage directions advice printed from time to time in the text of a play giving instructions or information to the actors, or on setting and special effects

Standard English the form of English most widely accepted as the conventional form

stanza a group or pattern of lines forming a verse

statistic a type of fact that refers to numerical data about a specific subject, 'Eight out of ten viewers gave this programme a five-star rating.'

style the characteristics of a text that make it different from another

subordinate clause a clause that is secondary to another part of the sentence

summarising the process of giving a brief statement or concise account of a topic, often based on a longer text

syllable a single unit of speech, either a whole word or one part of a word, e.g. 'eat' had one syllable but 'eaten' had two.

symbol something that represents something else, usually with meanings that are widely known (e.g. a dove as a symbol of peace)

synonym a word or phrase that is very similar in meaning to another, e.g. *bitter* and *acidic*

synthesising the process of drawing information from one text and putting it together with information from another and drawing conclusions.

theme an idea running through a work of literature or art

third person the narrative perspective that uses 'he' or 'she'

tone see **mood**

topic sentence a sentence that expresses the main idea of a paragraph, sometimes the first of the paragraph

voice the speaker or **narrator** of a poem or work of fiction. This persona is created in the speaker's mind, though sometimes it can seem close to the poet's or writer's own voice